THE RURBANITE

THE RURBANITE

living in the country without leaving the city

ALEX MITCHELL

PHOTOGRAPHY BY SARAH CUTTLE

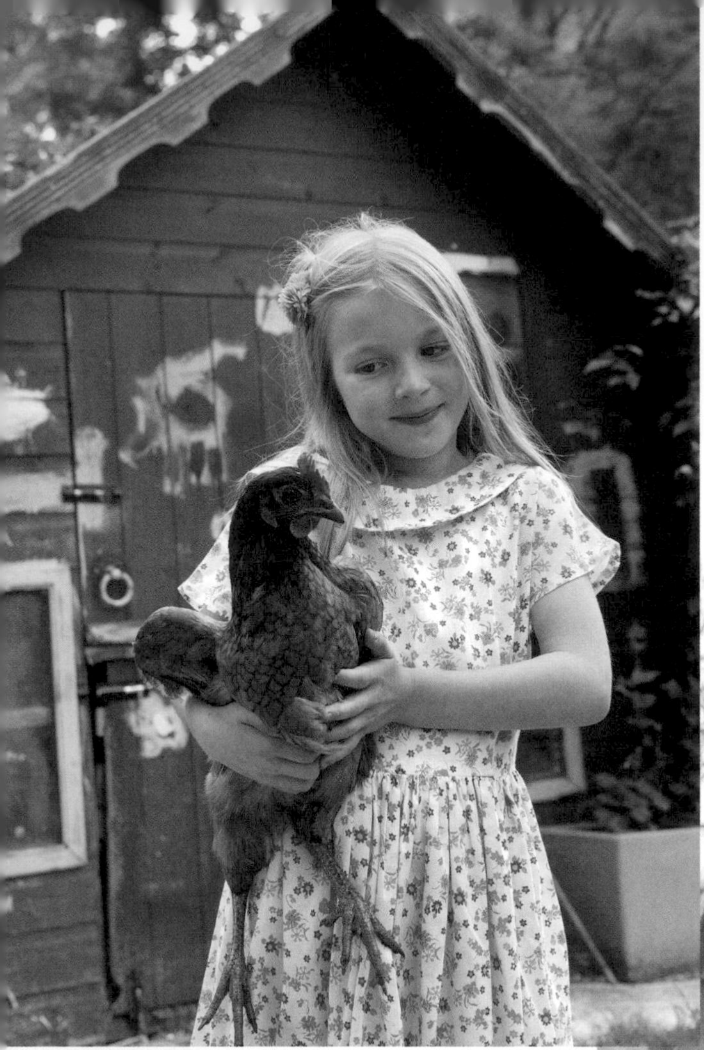

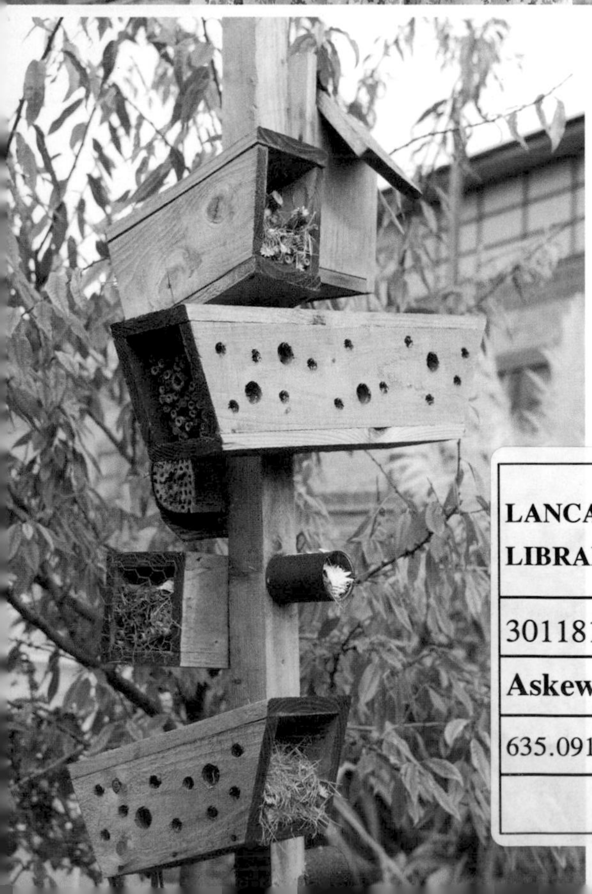

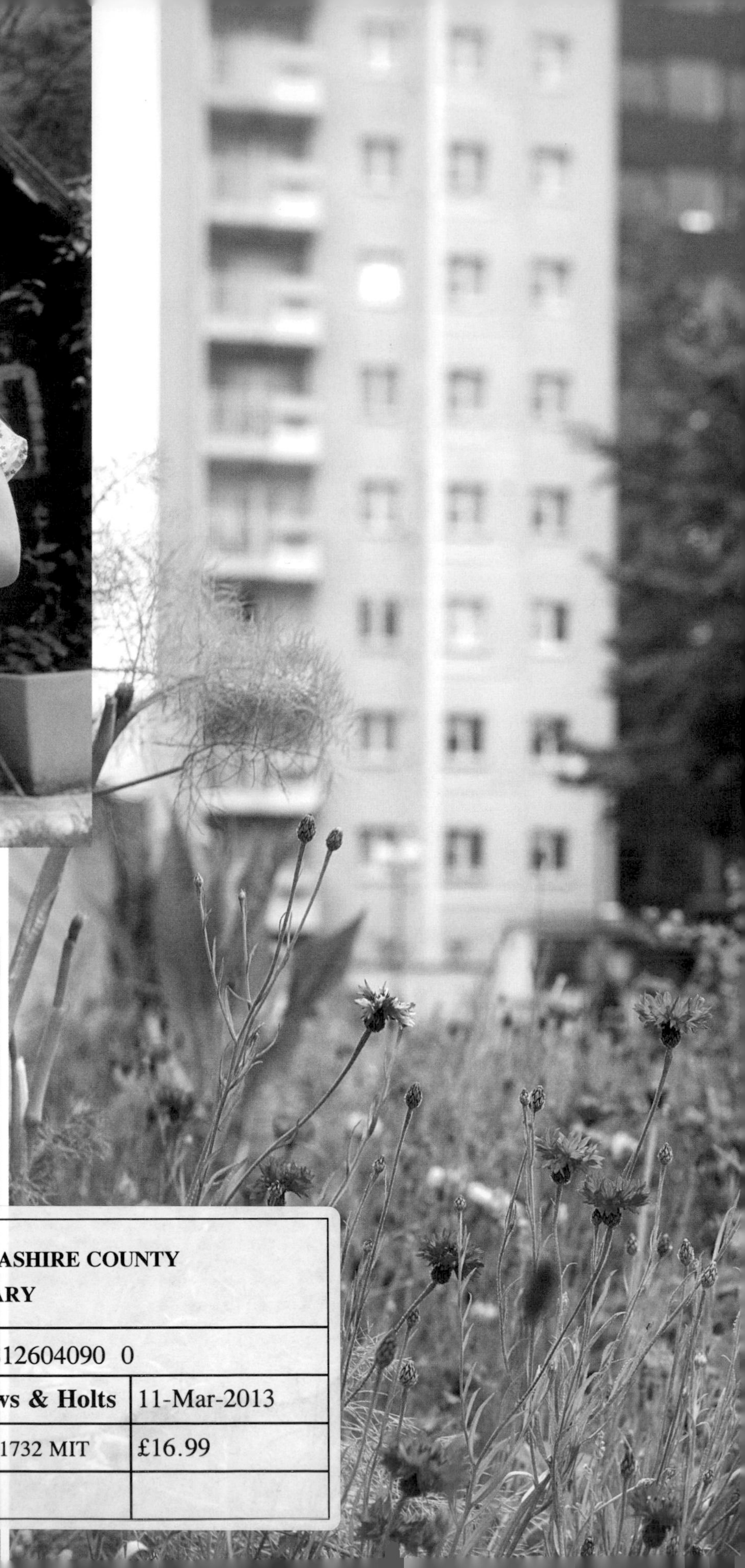

CONTENTS

INTRODUCTION

do you eye up that derelict patch of ground on your way to work and dream of turning it into a vegetable garden?

do you love living in the city but fantasise about keeping hens?

do you look at the weeds by the bus stop and wonder if they'd make a nice salad?

If you do, then you're a *rurbanite*. You have a passion for the countryside but no intention of leaving the city. Don't worry, you're not alone. You're part of a growing band of people who want the best of both worlds.

The countryside is pretty, but let's face it, has a few drawbacks. There are fewer people to talk to and they all look the same. Living in the country is less energy-efficient too: you spend more time driving the car and using expensive fuel because the distances between your home, friends, office and the shops are all greater. Your house is more likely to be detached so you spend more on heating. Everything is just a... little... bit... slow.

The city, of course, is never boring. But it has, traditionally, been grey not green. It's not for farms and livestock, it's for offices and apartment blocks, car exhausts and Tarmac. A change, however, is in the air. A growing band of rurbanites is getting in touch with the green side of the city. Want to grow vegetables but have no garden? No problem, get together with your neighbours and turn that derelict plot into a community garden. Like the idea of keeping hens and collecting their eggs in the morning? A city garden is the ideal place. Fancy yourself as a beekeeper? Honeybees love cities because there are fewer insecticides and lots of flowers: put a hive on your roof.

Urban homesteaders and city farmers are popping up like dandelions from Brooklyn to Berlin. They're meeting on beekeeping courses, learning to forage and harvesting unwanted local fruit. Sick of ugly, neglected, public planting schemes, they're taking matters into their own hands and greening their cities with seed bombs and bulbs. Neighbourhoods are reinvigorated as people meet through community gardens. Cities are once again seen as a chain of urban villages: we're falling back in love with the local.

We all know that a connection to nature is essential for a healthy frame of mind. We spend ever more time staring at screens, while 'nature-deficit disorder' – the quasi-medical condition coined by US author Richard Louv to describe the negative effect of spending less time outdoors – is blamed for everything from obesity to mental problems. Green spaces are vital for the health of city-dwellers, providing a refuge from pollution, a place for carbon-dioxide-absorbing trees and somewhere for weary urbanites to exercise. All around the world, city planners are looking for creative ways to bring some green to the urban sprawl. In Warsaw, Poland they are trying out prototypes of green tower blocks that mop up and filter pollution. Sao Paulo in Brazil boasts an office block clothed entirely in plants, rooting into porous concrete walls. Green roofs, too, can fight urban pollution, cut our fuel bills and manage rainwater.

'More than fifteen million people worldwide move from the countryside to the cities every year. It's expected that by 2050, 75 per cent of the world's population will live in cities — so there has never been a better time to plan how to make those cities appealing places to reside.'

We don't need a survey to tell us that we feel better when we stop for a moment and look at the flowers, listen to the birds or eat a homegrown carrot. As the world's urban population grows, city dwellers are seeking out and craving encounters with the natural world all the more.

Urban farms are sprouting all over the world: in Detroit, Chicago, Amsterdam and London. After food scandals and environmental scare stories about dwindling agricultural land, we've become suspicious of the traditional food supply system. We want more control over the food we eat, and what better way to do it than to grow the food ourselves? It tastes a lot better, too. But 'rurbanism' is not just about urban farming. We're also starting to realise how important cities can be for native wildlife, in some cases providing a refuge for species no longer at home in the agricultural factory of the countryside. We're putting green roofs on our garden sheds, learning to appreciate our native wildlife, protecting brownfield sites and planting to encourage bees.

Whether you just want to grow a few herbs and tomatoes or change the way you live in the city forever, this book will show you how to do it. Each chapter explores a different rurban action:

In 'Grow' you'll find out how to cultivate fruit and vegetables – on windowsills, in back gardens and allotments, plus how to attract urban wildlife and use guerrilla gardening in public spaces.

'Find' reveals the hidden gems alive in the verges, parks and pavements around you, from birds and insects to flowers and leaves for salads.

In 'Keep' you will find out how to raise bees, chickens, ducks and quail.

As you'll soon find out, city people really don't have to move to the country to meet nature head on. Which is a relief, because the coffee's better here.

grow... be a city farmer
be an urban homesteader
be a container grower
reclaim the street
benefit wildlife and the environment

Why buy fruit and vegetables flown in from thousands of miles away when you can grow your own crops here in the city? Why expect the countryside to provide all of our fresh food when we have plentiful wasted urban spaces that could be turned into productive farms? According to London's Capital Growth project, if all the available growing space in London was used, it could produce 26 per cent of the city's fruit and vegetables. Research in Germany reveals that the country has 36,000 hectares of rooftop space suitable for growing vegetables – roughly three times the space provided by all the greenhouses in the Netherlands. Yet we continue to truck in crops from miles away while potential urban growing spaces remain empty.

It takes just a bit of compost and a few skills to turn the most built-up city land into healthy farmland for potatoes, salads, tomatoes and more – and some dynamic people are pulling out the spades and demanding the chance to get stuck in. We want independence from the traditional food networks, and we want to reduce our ecological footprint by cutting food miles. We are growing salads on our windowsills and transforming back gardens with tomatoes, strawberries and potatoes. But we are not stopping at the front door: new community gardens, big and small, are sprouting in city neighbourhoods everywhere. These don't just produce crops – they give people a sense of belonging, too. Growing food connects us directly to the soil and to our locality. In a city that can feel enormous or overwhelming, it is grounding for people to know where their food comes from.

The job description 'urban farmer' has become commonplace as people in cities around the world wake up to the potential for urban agriculture. The American city of Detroit is showing what can be done. In the 1920s the city was one of the richest in the world, but collapsed when the car industry declined in the 1980s. Before long, an area the size of San Francisco had been overwhelmed by an army of weeds, with derelict factories, abandoned homes and deserted freeways. But in recent years, Detroit has witnessed a startling renaissance in the form of urban farming. Young people are reinvigorating the abandoned car lots with communal farms. Now fields of sweetcorn and squash grow in former suburban gardens and tractors carry hay down what were once busy city streets.

Youthful and dynamic, urban farmers passionately believe that we should be maximising the food-growing potential of our cities. Some take inspiration from Havana, Cuba, where the collapse of the Soviet bloc in 1991 forced a major agricultural effort in the city. Now, urban farms and gardens in Havana produce 70 per cent of the fresh fruit and vegetables consumed there. Hanoi in Vietnam is even more impressive, producing 80 per cent, while the densely populated city of Shanghai produces just over half.

The rooftops of Brooklyn are sprouting urban farms, run by hip young teams keen to spread their environmental message through blogs and Twitter. At Hayes Valley Farm, San Francisco's earthquake-damaged bridges are being turned into rows of brassicas and green manures. In England, the entire town of Todmorden has embraced an exciting collective food-growing experiment. The project's creator, Nick Green, told the *Telegraph*: 'Over the past five to ten years, food has suddenly become so much more interesting to people. It feels like the biggest social revolution since the Swinging Sixties.' Temporary edible gardens are springing up on brownfield sites in Berlin and London; the crops are grown in builders' bags and food crates so they can be moved when the developers turn up.

Some of these farms have commercial ambitions. In Chicago, an old meatpacking warehouse has been transformed into The Plant, an aquaponic vertical farm, where the nitrates in waste from tilapia fish feed vegetables growing hydroponically in vast trays inside the building. Both fish and crops are sold at a profit. Plans are under way to introduce a brewery – the spent grains will feed the fish – and an anaerobic digester to produce electricity and heat for the building. In the UK, the Urbivore project aims to grow 700 tonnes of food over the next five years. It is currently converting a 67-acre golf course into an urban farm in Stoke-on-Trent, an area in the West Midlands with the highest levels of obesity in Europe. Within sight of the UK's largest housing estate, the bunkers and greens are destined to become orchards, fields for livestock and a thriving market garden, with half of the produce to be sold to supermarkets, half to local outlets.

Other projects are more symbolic – the Farm:Shop in Dalston, east London, sits in a Victorian terrace house on a busy road. It has a polytunnel out the back, a mini aquaculture operation in the café and chickens on the roof. It wouldn't feed the residents of the street, but certainly makes you think. In Elephant and Castle, south London, land around an estate has been transformed into a mini meadow, with haymaking in high summer. Will the hay fill more than a garage? Probably not. Does it charm and inspire people? Definitely.

> 'Urban farmers in Havana produce 70 per cent of the fresh fruit and vegetables consumed in the city.'

BE A CITY FARMER

'It's not long before any shared garden, however modest, becomes a community hub where people meet to talk about more than food and flowers.'

City life can be a bit anonymous. Many of us shuffle from our front doors to our workplaces and then back again, barely noticing our neighbours. But more and more of us city types aren't satisfied with this disconnect, and we're showing it by breaking out of our own four walls, and digging holes.

With little, if any, growing space at home, we're looking around at the derelict lots, the scrubby patches of no-man's land, the rubbish-strewn bits we hurry past on the way home from work, and seeing potential for lettuces, tomatoes and beans. Once we mention our crazy ideas to others, we realise that people on our street feel just the same way. Before we know it, we've made a new garden, and lots of new friends. It's not long before any shared garden, however modest, becomes a community hub where people meet to talk about more than food and flowers.

It's a trend that can only grow as we change our working habits and spend more time at home. By 2020 there will be an overall decline in the number of people in Europe commuting to an office. In the next ten years, 50 per cent of workers in the USA are expected to be freelance. As we spend more time in our own neighbourhoods, it follows that we'll get to know our neighbours a little better.

There are loads of practical advantages to growing food in a shared space. It will probably be a bigger plot than you have at home, so you can really let your imagination run riot. The heavy work of setting up a garden is much easier as a team. There will always be someone else available to water when you're on holiday and, come harvest time, it's a great excuse for a party. But where to start? There are plenty of ways you can grow food beyond your own borders. Here are a few ideas...

the shared garden plot

You don't have a garden. But someone else does. So they let you cultivate some of their garden space with fruit and vegetables and, in return, they get lots of nice fresh tomatoes, salad and beans without having to do any hard work. What could be simpler? There is plenty of information on the internet about this kind of 'land share' or 'garden share' initiative. Just do an internet search for one then enter your postcode and get matched to a nearby garden.

Before you get clicking, here are a few pointers for successful garden sharing:

1. Before you commit, make sure you have the time to spare.

2. Know what you are doing, and if you don't, ask a more experienced gardener to help you. 'Growing in someone's garden is kind of like offering to decorate their house for free,' says Patti Kydd who runs the Grow Your Neighbour's Own garden-share scheme in Brighton and Hove, cities in the south of England that are decidedly short on garden space. 'Just because they're not paying anything doesn't mean they will forgive you messing it up!'

3. For garden owners, the more you get involved, the more you will get out of it. Plant the crops together and you'll not only make a potential new friend, but also end up with vegetables you actually want to eat.

RURBANITES: Mak Gilchrist and Will Sandy, the community gardeners, Brixton, London

The land at the end of Landor Road, Brixton in London used to be a nothing sort of place, a few compacted patches of earth, trampled by the people heading for the number 322 bus. But when a planning application was made to build houses on it, the local residents were galvanised into action. While talking in the pub, the conversation turned to the appearance of a lone sweetcorn plant that a mystery guerrilla gardener had added to the space. It got them thinking: why not turn the space into a community food garden instead?

Fashion model Mak Gilchrist, who has lived there for twenty-three years, and landscape architect Will Sandy were instrumental in turning the chat to reality, organising a clean-up day and asking people to donate plants and seeds. The garden, known as The Edible Bus Stop, is only a year old, yet the beds are full of both plants and volunteers digging out weeds and planting bulbs. Cabbages, tomatoes, strawberries and enormous kales now adorn the pavement and people can plant, weed or pick while they're passing by or waiting at the bus stop.

> *'I've lived here for twenty years, and I'd never spoken to anyone till I got involved with this garden.'*
> — Edible Bus Stop volunteer, Brixton, London

Last summer they had a street party and the café opposite made soup for everyone from the vegetables they had grown. They hope to roll out the concept across other bus stops in the city, starting with others on the same route.

Why a food garden? 'You can plant a rose and it looks beautiful,' says Will. 'But a tomato engages people, you can harvest and eat it together. One woman told me, 'I didn't know anyone before I got involved in this garden, and I've lived here for twenty years.' Mak agrees: 'Edibles are more inclusive. You can have a conversation over a tomato with a local West Indian granny and the banker just moved in down the road; that's not going to happen over a rose bush.'

Mak and Will's top tips to make a garden

1. 'Just dig it,' says Will. 'If you find a plot and start work on it, chances are the local authority will let you go ahead once they've seen what an amazing space you're making.'

2. 'Be inclusive – leave your egos aside.'

3. 'Remember it's not just about the gardening,' says Mak, 'it's about the community. Create other events that the garden is featured in, such as street parties or afternoon tea and cake. Sugar and alcohol are always good ways to get people together!'

the ignored plot

Every city has little bits of land that nobody seems to own. Who's responsible for them? Nobody's quite sure. They might be a couple of trampled flowerbeds at the end of your road in which nothing grows but beer cans and cigarette butts or a strip of land between your apartment block and the road. Local authorities may technically be responsible for the upkeep of these spaces, but their hearts don't really seem to be in it.

If you have a plot like this near your home, why not see if you can turn it into a food-growing space? See From Wasteland to Wonderland, page 21, for a suggested plan of action.

the 'awaiting development' plot

Cities are dotted with shabby patches of land waiting to be turned into something else, sometimes for many years. They might look unloved, with fly-tipped rubbish to prove it, but someone, somewhere has plans for these spaces, so any gardening on them will probably have to be temporary, and permission will have to be sought from the company or local authority who owns them. In many cases, local authorities are supportive of food-growing projects in these 'meanwhile spaces'. Even property developers can be supportive of temporary urban agriculture projects on sites earmarked for building. It's good publicity for them

LEFT: Neglected city areas such as this London roundabout have great potential for community gardening.

RIGHT: If you think the soil might be polluted, get around the problem by growing crops in raised beds.

after all. One such project, The Urban Orchard, saw a scrubby bit of land under the railway arches in London Bridge's hinterland transformed in 2010 into a green oasis of apple, pear, cherry and plum trees, all grown in pots and later rehomed with residents of the flats nearby.

Often former car parks or industrial sites, these spaces are usually concreted over, so planting has to be in raised containers. The benefit of this is that you don't have to worry about potential contaminants from the soil. It also means you can take your garden with you if you have to move on.

who owns it anyway? 5 steps to a new plot

So you've spotted some vacant or neglected land, and you're dreaming of turning it into a veg garden. Here's how you do it...

1. Ask around locally to find out the history of the site and discover who owns it. If no one knows, ask your local authority. Try to find an official there who knows, because in many cases, the local authority will be the site owner.
2. Start chatting to your neighbours about your idea and find out if people are behind it. You can do this face to face or by leafleting through letter boxes – talking is friendlier.
3. If you feel you have some good local support, call the site owner and discuss your plan with them. They might be supportive, or they might know of an alternative site that would work better.
4. Look on the internet for any local funding schemes that could help you with set-up costs and advice. London's Capital Growth scheme, for example, has supported almost 2,000 new growing spaces since 2009.
5. Before you start the garden, you will need a written agreement to be drawn up between you and the landowner. Depending on how risk averse the landowner is, you may also need insurance. Local authority or funding groups can help you with this.

from wasteland to wonderland

Congratulations, you have control of a patch of wild weeds and rubbish. But before you get busy with the loppers and the spades, a few things to consider...

Leave some weeds

It might look like an ugly jungle of brambles and nettle to you, but this patch of waste ground could be a valuable brownfield site (See Grow for Wildlife and the Environment, page 92). Butterflies lay eggs on those nettles, bees drink nectar from the bramble flowers and birds eat the berries. Before you start hacking away, agree on an area that can be left wild and do just that. You'll have lovely nettle tops to make soup from in the spring (see How to Make Nettle Soup, page 129).

Is my soil safe?

Urban waste grounds can contain pollutants. Some sites may have been used as garages or workshops. Local authorities may have records of what the site was previously used for and you can send off for a soil analysis (home tests are not reliable enough). However, these soil tests are costly and information is often hard to come by, so most people tend to bypass the issue by growing in raised beds or containers with a weed-suppressing membrane at the base to prevent roots going down to the soil below. This removes any anxiety about potential soil contamination.

tip If you're growing in raised beds, timber can often be found for free in building skips. Scaffolding boards are ideal. For each bed you'll need three equal length boards, four short corner posts, a saw, a mallet, a hammer and some nails. Saw one of the boards in half to make the ends. Then arrange the boards into position, setting them about 3cm deep into the soil for stability. With the mallet, hammer a post into each corner then nail the boards to the corner posts to make a rigid bed. When working out the dimensions of a raised bed, bear in mind that you should be able to reach the centre from each side without treading on the soil. Otherwise you'll trample your crops. The length is less important.

water, water, anywhere?

Crops need water, but many public urban spots don't have it on tap. If there is a roof on or near the garden, save water running off it by fitting a water butt at the end of the downpipe. Get talking to neighbours and ask if they would mind letting you run a hose from their garden tap. In the York Rise estate in north London, the communal garden is regularly watered by a hose dropped down from a third-floor bathroom window. If you can't find a nearby water source, consider planting drought-tolerant crops (see Not-so-Thirsty Crops, page 32) or make simple watering systems such as the one below.

how to MAKE A HASSLE-FREE WATERING SYSTEM

This simple system is ideal for communal urban gardens since it seriously takes the fuss out of watering a fairly large area of crops, and is particularly useful when water is in short supply. You can find everything in a DIY or pound store.

you will need

A sturdy bucket

A drill

A Stanley knife

A plastic tap (such as those for water butts)

4 or 5 bricks (or similar) to stand the bucket on

A length of seep or soaker hosing, perforated hose or garden hose with holes made in the side

1 plug or stopper for the end of the hose

30 minutes

when to do it: all year round

how to do it

Using the biggest drill but you can find, drill a hole in the side of the bucket near the bottom. Then use the knife to enlarge the hole so the tap fits snugly into it. Do this carefully, little by little, as the water will leak out if the hole is too big. Stand the bucket on the bricks, then attach the hose to the tap and lay the hose on the soil surface, snaking it around your plants so that it is near to each one. You can bury the hose slightly under the soil if you like. Put the plug in the open end of the hose. Fill the bucket with water. Slowly the water will seep out of the holes in the hose into the soil around the plants' roots, just where they need it most. The bucket will catch rainwater too.

5
ESSENTIAL THINGS

FOR A SHARED GARDEN

Compost bins (see How to Make a Compost Bin for Free, page 45)

A communal seating area, even if it's just some logs laid on the ground

Defined beds

A nearby water source, even if it's just a friendly neighbour's bathroom tap or a water butt

An area left wild to encourage wildlife (see Grow for Wildlife and the Environment, page 92)

5
LESS ESSENTIAL BUT LOVELY THINGS

FOR A SHARED GARDEN

A pond

Somewhere to store garden tools and other equipment

A covered area such as a pagoda to shelter rain-sodden volunteers

A barbecue – nothing brings people together better than grilled food; throw on some just-picked sweetcorn for perfection

A logbook in a zip-lock plastic bag to record what has been sown and harvested

tip It's up to you how you decide to share your harvest, but most communal gardens follow an informal system for dividing the spoils of their labours – the more work you put in, the more crops you take home. This tends to work surprisingly well.

5 best crops for a shared garden

All of these highly productive crops are perfect for growing in shared plots, not only because they require little attention once established, but also because you will all get something to take home.

Kale

Kales are the unsung heroes of the vegetable world because they produce leaves for months on end. One plant of Cavolo Nero (or Black Tuscan kale) can sustain you from early autumn to mid spring, while even less prolific varieties such as red-midribbed Red Russian and burgundy Redbor will keep churning out the leaves. Chuck it into soups, stir-fry and sprinkle with Parmesan or steam it and serve with plenty of butter with roast meats. If you pick the leaves very young they are mild enough to eat raw in salads too.

Even on a biting winter day, you can pick this brassica, its leaves veined with frost and its statuesque form laughing in the face of the cold. It is also far less susceptible to caterpillar and snail damage than other brassicas such as cabbage, though watch out for pigeons (old DVDs strung up nearby are said to deter them).

Kale is best sown in small pots in late spring and then transplanted to a sunny spot about 30cm apart in mid summer. It likes a fertile soil, where garden compost or well-rotted manure has been added. Be sure to plant firmly – the test is to pull a leaf after planting. If it breaks before you uproot the plant, it's planted firmly enough. If you harvest leaves from the bottom of the stem up as and when you need them you should be picking from early autumn right through to mid spring. At this point the plants will produce flowering shoots which, if picked before the yellow flowers open, are deliciously sweet and crunchy eaten raw and taste just like sprouting broccoli if lightly steamed.

• See page 73 for tips on growing kale in containers

Chard

Pretty, productive and downright unkillable, chard (right) is arguably the ultimate grow-your-own crop. Forget to water it and it bounces back; cut its outer leaves and it provides more with each plant producing for at least four months. Expect to be taking bagfuls home from a shared garden on a regular basis – but get it home fast or it will wilt before you can get through the front door, a characteristic that keeps it out of regular supermarkets. Like spinach's more muscly brother, chard has a robust flavour when cooked that goes brilliantly with butter or cheese sauce. Or you can eat young leaves raw when they have a sweet beetrooty crunch. With their searing, almost fluorescent pink and yellow stems, it's no wonder that the Bright Lights or Rainbow varieties have become an allotment staple, providing a splash of colour. The white stemmed Swiss chard is relatively demure, though just as tasty.

Sow chard from mid spring right through to early autumn, either in small pots or direct into cultivated garden soil or larger containers. Space plants about 30cm apart. If you protect plants over winter with some horticultural fleece they should keep cropping right through until the following spring. Watch out for slugs and snails in the early stages and later for leaf miners, tiny larvae that make tunnels inside the leaves causing dead, brown patches. Either remove individual leaves or squish the larvae inside the leaf with your finger and cut out the affected parts.

• See page 73 for tips on growing chard in containers

Salad potatoes

This is a great crop for communal growing because the effort of planting is tiny and the harvests are substantial – unlike, say, baby salad leaves, you can make a meal from a bagful of spuds after a morning's work at the plot. You can grow maincrop (large) potatoes that stay in the ground until the leaves yellow in autumn, but in the city where space is tight it makes more sense to focus on the salad spuds, known as first or second earlies, not only because you can taste the difference when you grow them yourself, but because you harvest them far earlier, so they take up space for less time.

Just-dug salad potatoes have an unmistakable sweetness. Once you've tasted them, any other potato seems rather lacklustre. Whether in a spring salad with early beetroot and baby broad beans or just steamed with fresh mint, they are unbeatable. They're also more expensive in the shops. For super-quick crops, ready after 10 weeks, Swift or Rocket will deliver, though Orla, Anya, Lady Christl or Charlotte probably have the edge flavour-wise, with a firm, nutty sweetness. Expect to harvest about 20 tubers from each potato you plant.

If you have space, try a few maincrops or leave earlies in the ground until the end of summer to let them bulk up – the burgundy Red Duke of York is as delicious as a baking potato as it is as a salad spud. And why stop at red when you could be growing black or blue potatoes? You won't be harvesting maincrops such as Shetland Black, Vitelotte, Congo or Salad Blue until late summer, but their chestnutty butteriness is worth the wait. They make unique chips too.

Start your potatoes off by 'chitting' them from late winter – placing them on a windowsill inside so that their shoots can start growing. Potatoes grow best in fertile, moist, well-cultivated soil in a sunny spot, so mulch the ground with a good layer (at least 15cm) of garden compost or well-rotted manure the previous autumn (if you miss this, mulch in early spring instead).

By mid spring, when the frosts are nearly over, you can plant out your potatoes. Choose a sunny spot and dig a narrow trench (about a trowel's width) roughly 20cm deep, scattering a few slug pellets along the bottom to stop these pests tunnelling into your tubers. Each trench should be about 60cm apart. Place your potatoes along the trench about 30cm apart, with the chitted shoots uppermost. If you don't have room for a trench, just make individual holes for each potato about 20cm deep and 30cm apart.

Backfill the trench with soil and water well. Once the green shoots (the haulm) poke up through the soil, they are susceptible to frost so cover them with newspaper overnight if it is forecast. When the haulm is about 30cm tall, 'earth it up' by dragging soil from around it so that only a few centimetres of haulm are still visible. This keeps weeds down, protects the shoots from frost and increases the yield. The key to a good potato harvest is plenty of water. Soak the plants thoroughly at least twice a week in hot weather.

Knowing when first or second early potatoes are ready is a mixture of experience and guesswork. Some are ready when they start flowering, other varieties never flower. As a general rule, first earlies are ready to harvest from early summer, about 12 weeks after planting, while second earlies take about 14 weeks. Have an exploratory, careful dig around with a handfork before digging up a whole plant. If the potatoes are the size of hens' eggs, they are ready.

A LAZY POTATO BED

Potatoes are particularly good as a 'starter crop' for previously uncultivated land, so if your back garden has been a weed-strewn jungle for the past three years, they're a good choice. Not only are they delicious and highly productive, they also have a nice habit of preparing the soil for any future crop, saving you the hassle. Grow them in the way I'm about to describe and you won't have to water them, weed them or earth them up because the plastic and cardboard will suppress weeds and light and keep moisture in the soil, while allowing rain to get in. All these layers do, however, make a lovely habitat for slugs, which can tunnel into your tubers, so a few slug pellets added to the planting holes are a good idea.

Although the black plastic is initially conspicuous, potato plants soon cover it with their sprawling leaves so this isn't even one to hide behind the compost bins. You'll get a decent crop of potatoes and the bonus of lovely crumbly soil for your next crop.

you will need

A patch of uncultivated ground (in a garden or allotment)

Chitted seed potatoes (ideally 'first early' or 'second early' – see varieties opposite)

Cardboard that, when flattened, covers the growing area

Black plastic or landscape fabric (sometimes called weed-suppressing membrane) from garden centres

Organic slug pellets

Scissors

A hand trowel

A watering can

An hour and a half

Planks of wood, bricks or stones to anchor the plastic

when to do it

Early to mid spring

how to do it

If you are planting in a grass area, first mow or cut the grass, leaving the cuttings on the surface. If planting in weedy soil, chop down vigorous weeds to ground level. Water the area thoroughly. Using your trowel, make holes about 15cm deep, 10cm wide and 30cm apart. If the ground is hard, just make as deep a hole as you can. Add a few slug pellets to each hole, then pop a chitted seed potato into each one and cover it with soil and grass cuttings. Water again thoroughly. Now cut the flattened cardboard into sections and lay these on the ground so that they cover the area, leaving a 10cm square gap in the cardboard above each planted potato so it can grow unimpeded. Water the cardboard thoroughly until it is soggy. Finally, cover the wet cardboard with black plastic or landscape fabric, weighing it down with stones, bricks, wood or soil.

As the potatoes grow they will make little hills in the plastic or fabric: make holes to let them through. Watering should not be necessary since the plastic and cardboard will keep moisture in the soil, but check occasionally to make sure. If using landscape fabric you may need to water more regularly since it is not so effective at retaining moisture.

Harvest 'earlies' about 13 weeks after planting by simply removing the plastic and cardboard and digging them up when you want them. You can either remove the cardboard or dig it into the soil.

Courgettes and squashes

To grow well, these strong, robust plants need sun, good water-retaining soil with plenty of organic matter, space and lots of water. If you can provide all these, you'll be rewarded handsomely. The more courgettes and summer squashes you pick, the more they produce, a fact that has given them a reputation for providing gluts. But in a shared garden, they're a win-win, since no one person is going to have a chance to get tired of them.

Winter squashes, which have hard skins and so can last for months after harvesting, tend to be slightly less prolific but are a lot of fun to grow, from the sweet Uchiki Kuri or Red Onion Squash with its fiery lantern fruit to the bizarre Spaghetti squash which has pasta-like strands inside. Both are climbers and will soon cover a pergola or trellis. Butternut varieties tend to need a warm climate to ripen reliably so bear this in mind when choosing. Pick winter squashes in early autumn and leave them in the sun to cure for a few days so the skin can harden before storing.

If you want a classic green courgette, Defender is a good choice. The Italian variety Romanesco has striking stripes and the yellow Soleil is irresistibly cheerful looking. Round varieties such as Eight Ball are good for smaller spaces. As for summer squashes, the patty pan types such as buttercup yellow Sunburst or Custard White are beautiful and delicious picked small and steamed whole. But for wow factor, try climbing squash Tromboncino or Serpente, a curly whirly wonder that's great eaten young like a courgette or left to cure for the winter.

Sow courgettes and squashes about 2cm deep in small pots in mid spring and transplant them in early summer to a sunny spot in which compost or manure has been incorporated, spacing plants about 40cm apart. Climbing plants should be tied into supports as they grow to make the most of your space. Feed courgettes and squashes fortnightly once they start to flower with a high-potash feed such as a tomato feed or liquid seaweed. Wormery tea is also beneficial. The flowers can be battered and stuffed with feta or ricotta. Courgettes in particular are susceptible to powdery mildew, a fungal disease that can weaken the plant and make the surface of the leaves look as though they are dusted with talcum powder. It is caused by overcrowding and dry roots, so keep well watered and cut off affected leaves.

Garlic

A great plant-and-walk-away crop, garlic is not only easy to grow, but ideal for a shared garden because a little goes a very long way. However big your band of volunteers, everyone should be able to take at least one head of garlic home.

All you have to do to grow garlic is to split a head into individual cloves in the spring or autumn and plant them about 15cm apart in cultivated soil pointy end up so the tips are just below the surface. Garlic likes a sunny spot and isn't too fussy about soil though dig in some grit if you have a particularly heavy clay. And that's it. Each clove will miraculously turn into a new head of garlic.

Keep well watered, particularly in early summer as the bulbs begin to form. Depending on the variety, garlic is ready to harvest from early summer when the leaves start to turn yellow (have an investigatory dig to see if they're big enough). Dry the heads well in the sunshine for a few days until the skin turns papery; they will then keep in a well-ventilated larder for many months.

Don't be tempted to plant supermarket garlic since it might not be a variety suited to your climate – instead buy from a garden centre or specialist supplier. Solent Wight, ready in mid summer, is a great long-storing variety that will keep for up to a year, while the mild-flavoured short-storing varieties Purple Wight and Early Wight are ready by late spring and should be eaten within a few weeks.

• See also chillies (page 70), runner & French beans (page 57), tomatoes (page 51), herbs (pages 34–36), lettuce and other salads (pages 56-57), rocket (page 32), Jerusalem artichokes (page 32), raspberries (page 48), kai lan (page 57), globe artichokes (page 58), radishes (page 70), spring onions (page 70)

'The more courgettes and summer squashes you pick, the more they produce – perfect for a shared garden.'

RURBANITES: Marco Clausen and Robert Shaw, mobile urban farmers, Berlin

In Kreuzberg in downtown Berlin, next to a roaring roundabout and overshadowed by apartment blocks, there's a brightly painted sign. 'Today and every day,' it says, 'harvesting fresh vegetables and herbs. No kidding!' A few steps on and you enter Prinzessinnengarten, a 6,000m square garden and community hub where homegrown salad is being served from a converted shipping container. A few years before, this was a wasteland strewn with rubbish and broken glass, the site of a department store that had been destroyed by bombs in the Second World War and left abandoned for 65 years.

It was a trip to Cuba that first inspired Robert Shaw, a filmmaker who knew next to nothing about gardening, to set up an urban farm. 'By accident he discovered the so-called "agricultura urbana",' says Marco, left, who runs the farm with him. 'He was amazed.' Back in Berlin, the duo spotted a potential location – a patch of wasteland downtown – and leased it from the city on a temporary basis. They put an advert in the local paper asking for people to come and help them clear the site and 150 volunteers turned up.

Now, lines of milk cartons, builders' bags, bakers' crates and rice sacks – adding up to about 800 square metres of growing space – stretch into the distance, all filled with crops, from spinach and leeks to cabbages, aubergines and tomatoes. Potatoes sprout from rice sacks and milk cartons froth with lettuces. Volunteers and paid workers turn the 500 different crops into soups, pizzas and salads from a converted shipping container that serves as the garden café. Every few weeks, a table is laid with a white tablecloth and a garden dinner is served, for a hundred people.

'The municipality wants to sell the place,' says Marco, 'so we don't know how long we can stay here.' Luckily, this isn't so daunting. These crates full of crops can easily be loaded on to pallets and moved to a new location. Somewhere in Berlin the garden will live on.

> 'A few years before, this was a wasteland strewn with rubbish and broken glass.'

5 not-so-thirsty crops

All of these crops are fairly drought-tolerant so are ideal if you don't have a handy water source at your garden or can't get to the site on a daily basis. They will, however, need watering until they get established.

Rocket

This peppery salad leaf comes in two types – salad rocket, which is over within a season, and the spikier, hotter wild rocket, plants of which can grow into bushes and last for several years. If sowing in autumn or early spring, choose salad rocket, but for summer sowings go for the wild form since it is less likely to bolt in hot weather. Sow both about 1cm deep and 5cm apart in rows roughly 15cm apart in sunny or shady spots. Re-sow salad rocket every couple of weeks for a lasting supply. Watch out for slugs and snails. If your leaves become peppered with tiny holes like gunshot, it's probably flea beetle, a little black jumping beetle. The damage is cosmetic, but if you are bothered by the holes, cover your crop with horticultural fleece. Harvest by snipping just above the smallest new leaf.

Beetroot

Sow this root crop generously and you won't regret it, whether you're crunching into its raw leaves in salads or biting into the meltingly soft, sweet roasted roots, so perfect with feta or goat's cheese. Sow beetroot from early spring to mid summer, about 2cm deep and 5cm apart in rows roughly 20cm apart. Thin seedlings to 10cm apart. It does best in a sunny spot though will tolerate partial shade. Watch for slugs and snails in the early stages.

As for varieties, choose Chioggia for impact on the plate – it has striking pink and white concentric rings when sliced – or Bull's Blood for impact in the garden, its deep burgundy leaves are good in salads (remember, though, to leave a few on the plant so the root can develop). Other excellent varieties include the orange Burpee's Golden, Pablo and Boltardy. Harvest when golf-ball sized (about 12 weeks after sowing) and boil or roast for maximum sweetness. Or why not try beetroot carpaccio – sliced paper thin and eaten raw with a good salad dressing? A mix of red, striped and orange varieties makes for a dazzling plateful. Don't forget to take a few young leaves for salads.

New Zealand spinach

Despite its name, this is unrelated to spinach, but when the triangular green leaves are steamed they taste pretty much the same. Otherwise known as Tetragon, it's a great crop for hot, dry summers since, unlike regular spinach, it won't bolt if it dries out, but keeps growing up to 60cm tall and trailing over the ground, making it useful ground cover since it will keep weeds down. You can pick the small, fuzzy leaves again and again and treat them in the kitchen just as you would normal spinach, adding to pasta, or serving as a side vegetable. It's a perennial, but not frost-tolerant so will probably last until winter kicks in.

New Zealand spinach likes a warm soil so either wait until mid to late spring to sow direct in a sunny spot in the garden or sow in small pots inside from early spring and transplant later. The knobbly seeds are best soaked overnight before sowing to aid germination. Sow about 1cm deep and 10cm apart, thinning plants to roughly 30cm apart once they have established. Water well after sowing – it is tolerant to a bit of neglect once it has got going. No need to feed.

Jerusalem artichokes

Another plant-and-walk-away crop, requiring nothing from you but the planting of the knobbly tubers about 12cm deep and 30cm apart in the spring. The less knobbly variety Fuseau is the one to go for since it doesn't take long to peel. They make a sublime, velvety soup, or are delicious roasted.

Jerusalem artichokes thrive in a sunny spot but will tolerate partial shade and, like potatoes, will break up heavy soils so are a great crop for a new plot that hasn't yet seen much cultivation. Since they can grow up to 3 metres tall, they are also useful as a windbreak providing shelter for other crops. By late summer they will be crowned by pretty yellow flowers, a reminder that they are related to the sunflower. Dig up the plentiful tubers as and when you want them any time from late summer through the winter – they will be fine under ground. Cut the thick stems down to the ground when they turn brown in the autumn – they can be useful to keep as supports for other plants.

'Rocket and beetroot – ideal crops if water is not easily accessible.'

HERBS

Many herbs like a bit of neglect – go for a short walk on a dry Mediterranean hillside and you'll see see thyme and rosemary thriving in the dust and stones. Other herbs, such as basil, mint and parsley like a moister, richer soil, but all herbs are relatively low-maintenance, and since you only ever need a few leaves in the kitchen, they're the perfect choice for a communal space when you need enough to go round. There are other pluses to this group too – they generally look very pretty, from mounds of flowering silver thyme edging a path to rosemary tumbling over a raised bed. And there's little that's more relaxing in an edible garden than wandering around crushing leaves of oregano, sage or mint in your fingers as you go – instant aromatherapy.

All plants need watering when first sown or transplanted and herbs are no exception, but once they are established, you need only water them sparingly unless there is a drought or they are planted in pots.

5 easily neglected herbs

All of these Mediterranean herbs like dry, free-draining soil. If you have a heavy soil, add plenty of grit before planting. If planting in a raised bed or large container, it's a good idea to position them near the edge where drainage is best. All need full sun to do best.

Rosemary

This makes a handsome plant, its needle-like leaves held on the bush all year round and its blue flowers a magnet for pollinating insects such as the delightful spring hairy-footed flower bee. Rosemary grows to a considerable size and can live for many years so plant in a minimum 30cm diameter pot unless you choose a compact form. Buy plants rather than growing from seed and trim to keep it in shape after flowering – leaves can be harvested all year round, the perfect partner for lamb and other meats as well as roast potatoes. The classic *rosmarinus officinalis* is a good upright choice though if you want something that trails, try the prostrate form. There are also pink or white flowered varieties. Harvest by snipping off sections of branch and don't be afraid to hack it back if it gets out of hand. Rosemary is forgiving.

Thyme

To grow well, the delectable smelling thyme needs a very free-draining soil and lots of sun so add plenty of grit if planting in a container or heavy soil and give it your hottest spot. Choose from common or garden thyme (*thymus vulgaris*) for a pretty dark green plant with mauve flowers, or the variegated Silver Queen, lemon thyme or broad-leaved thyme (*thymus pulegioides*), which has generous-sized leaves and so goes furthest in the kitchen. Best grown from a plant rather than seed, thyme is frost hardy and will live for many years given the right conditions, but will become straggly if you don't cut it back hard after flowering. Try it in a hanging basket or windowbox or let it trail down the side of a raised bed.

Oregano

This shallow-rooted herb is more than happy in containers such as hanging baskets or windowboxes for several years and, if planted in a bed, will sprawl all over the place, dotted with pretty white flowers which bees adore. The leaves smell spicy and delicious when you rub them between your fingers and bring a note of authenticity to Italian and Greek dishes. Easiest grown from a plant rather than seed. After flowering, cut it back so it doesn't become too straggly.

Sage

Like rosemary, this furry-leaved hardy perennial can grow into a huge bush so bear this in mind when you plant your diminutive potted specimen (like many herbs this is one to grow from a small plant, rather than seed). The classic variety *salvia officinalis* is vigorous and lovely, while the relatively slow-growing purple-leaved sage brings a dash of colour to the border. If grown in a container, make sure it is at least 30cm in diameter to give the plant room to grow. Pick individual leaves – a little goes a long way – and add them chopped to buttery pasta or serve with meats such as pork, chicken or duck.

French tarragon

It doesn't look like much, with its rather wispy, floppy leaves and dull green colour, but this unassuming herb punches above its weight in the kitchen, the vital component of velvety béarnaise sauce and the perfect partner for chicken. Buy plants in spring, making sure it is the French not the inferior Russian variety. Only half hardy, French tarragon is best grown in pots so you can bring it into the house, conservatory or greenhouse in late autumn to protect it from winter weather. Grown this way a plant can live for several years.

tip Parsley and rosemary can be harvested all year round, but oregano, sage and thyme become bare or slow to a standstill in winter. Preserve a few leaves by picking at the height of summer and drying. Chives, mint, tarragon and basil can be chopped, mixed with butter and lemon juice and frozen for herby butters.

5 herbs for moister soils

These need a richer, moisture-retaining soil and can tolerate some shade. They don't like being waterlogged, though, so water before midday to allow the ground to dry out before temperatures drop in the evening. If grown in the ground they don't require feeding with compost or liquid feeds, but potted herbs like a weekly feed of liquid seaweed or wormery tea from spring to autumn. Use a soil-based compost such as John Innes no. 3 in containers.

Basil

This sweet herb is so good thrown on to pizzas, whizzed up into pesto or strewn on to chopped tomato on garlicky bruschetta. Sow in mid spring in 7.5cm pots, five seeds per pot. Once they have germinated, thin to the three strongest seedlings. In early summer, tranplant these as a clump to larger containers or garden soil in a sun-drenched spot. Sweet Genovese is the classic Italian basil, but a purple form is well worth adding. You could also try the more aniseedy Thai basil, the perfect ingredient for pad thais and other noodle dishes. African basil is a perennial so will last through winter if you bring it inside. Harvest by pinching out the tops of the stems with your fingers – this encourages them to sprout lower down.

Coriander

Another herb to sow liberally since, once snipped, it won't re-sprout. Choose a 'leaf' variety for maximum harvest and sow in garden soil or containers about 3cm apart from mid spring onwards. Coriander doesn't like being transplanted so sow it where you are going to harvest it. Re-sow every three weeks for a constant supply. This herb is also particularly good when grown as a microgreen (see page 75).

Mint

Plant this vigorous, prolific herb in a container or its roots will soon colonise your entire garden. That aside, it's a marvellous herb since it will grow well even in shade. If growing in a garden bed, plant in a 30cm plastic pot and sink into the ground making sure the rim of the pot stands proud of the soil level. Cut with abandon since it readily re-sprouts and add leaves to new potatoes, summer cocktails or simply hot water for a refreshing digestif. You can find garden mint (*mentha sativa*) or spearmint (*mentha spicata*) easily in garden centres but it's fun to waste a pleasant half hour browsing the seemingly endless varieties available from a specialist herb supplier – from Moroccan Mint to Pineapple, Grapefruit and Ginger. Black peppermint makes arguably the best tea, spearmint or Moroccan the finest mint sauce.

Mint is best grown from plants rather than seed. Plant any time from spring to autumn. Chopping the stems back by half in mid summer induces a fresh growth of shoots. When the stems turn brown in late autumn cut them to the ground – the plant will re-sprout in the spring. If you want fresh mint over winter, dig up a small section of root in the autumn, potting it up and bring it inside.

Chives

Purple pom-pom flowers and a generous supply of mild oniony leaves make this a must-have. It is also very amenable to being divided so you can build up a large supply from just one initial plant. Simply dig up in spring, split the rootball in half with your fingers and plant each half in a separate hole. To harvest, snip leaves to about 2cm off the ground and they will keep growing. This establishes much more quickly if you buy a plant rather than grow from seed.

Parsley

Since it has a long taproot, parsley needs a deep soil or large container to grow well. Other than that it is extremely unfussy. It will grow happily in shade or sun and, as long as you keep the soil moist, it should thrive. The only other thing to remember is that parsley is a biennial, meaning it lives for two years. Therefore it's best to re-sow every year to avoid a parsley gap. Sow the slow-germinating seeds on the surface of compost in small pots or modules in mid spring and transplant about 30cm apart when big enough to handle. Harvest by hacking at will, it will re-sprout magnanimously. French parsley is arguably best for cooking though the dwarf curled form makes a pretty and well-behaved edging to pathways.

INSPIRATION: Vacant Lot, Shoreditch

The paved area at the base of the Pitfield Estate in east London was originally a playground, but the swings and roundabout had been cleared away many years before the neglected spot was given a new lease of life. Since 2007, it has been flourishing with potatoes, beans, tomatoes, salad and marigolds. They're all growing in builders' bags, laid out on the tarmac and positively brimming with crops and flowers. Every resident of the housing estate has a bag to tend, to grow anything they like. Some grow flowers, swathes of lobelia and towering sunflowers. Others grow Oriental salad greens, strawberries or herbs. When they're not watering their crops, the residents have barbecues here or just sit in the sun. They help each other out by watering each other's crops. What was an eyesore, a blank nothingness in the midst of a built-up area, is now a social hub and larder for fresh food. The brainchild of the social regeneration project What If:, this garden is just one of many allotment spaces developing in inner-city London to give vacant and neglected spaces around housing estates new life.

tip Make your builders' bag beautiful. Plants will hide the white plastic surprisingly quickly – especially if you plant trailing tomatoes, herbs, nasturtiums or strawberries around the edge – but if you want to disguise the man-made look, use rolls of bamboo, willow or reed fencing from any garden centre. Plant tall beans and sunflowers to draw the eye upwards. The smaller 50kg bags make ideal containers for potatoes (see opposite). Roll the sides down to 30cm when planting and then roll up in stages, adding more compost to earth up the potatoes as they grow. You will end up with a tall bag bulging with potatoes like a Christmas stocking.

how to GROW FOOD IN A BUILDERS' BAG

Builders' bags make fantastic growing containers. They are made of woven polypropylene, they're extremely cheap, light to carry and perfect on concrete or where chemicals may have contaminated the soil. The enormous 1-tonne bags are ideal for large-scale community projects and will easily hold a fruit tree with other crops around it. Smaller 50kg-bags are great for domestic spaces and crops such as tomatoes or salads. The 1-tonne bags can take a lot of compost so don't feel you have to fill them to the top to start with – an initial compost depth of 30–40cm is enough. Just roll down the sides of the bag to the right depth – you can always add more compost later. The bags are durable and if you add manure or garden compost every growing season they will keep producing year after year.

you will need

A 1000kg (1-tonne) builders' bag, sides rolled down to 30cm in height

3 builders' buckets of crocks (enough to make a 5cm layer in the bottom of the bag) – polystyrene chunks, gravel, broken-up pots or rubble

200l of multipurpose compost, ideally containing 50l of well-rotted manure or garden compost to get crops off to a good start

A selection of fruit and vegetable crops such as a dwarf apple, pear or plum tree, strawberries, tomatoes, dwarf French beans, salads and herbs

1 hour

when to do it

Spring to late summer, though bare-rooted fruit trees can be planted over winter

how to do it

Place your bag in its final position, bearing in mind that it will be pretty heavy once you have added the compost. If you're planting multiple bags, be sure to leave enough space to walk comfortably between them. Add the crocks and then the compost. Plant the fruit tree in the centre of the bag and the other plants around it. Strawberries are best planted around the edge so the fruits can trail over the sides. There is no need to make drainage holes since the woven plastic lets water through, but if the compost gets waterlogged, make about six holes in the sides near the bottom with scissors or a knife.

BE AN URBAN HOMESTEADER

'It's a form of idealism which is more integrated and grounded than the escapist fantasies of the 1970s. There's less nudity, too...' Kelly Coyne, urban homesteader

If you're lucky enough to have a garden or allotment in the city, you are sitting on a potential treasure trove of fresh food. You can have raised beds and compost heaps. You can plant fruit trees, grapevines and rows of potatoes. You can grow enough food to make jam, jellies and chutneys to store over winter. You might even have room for a few hens or a beehive (see pages 145–153 and 158–167). In short, you can have your own little farm in the city.

You'd be in good company these days. Urbanites across the world are reconnecting with the little bits of land they own out the back. We're wanting more from our gardens these days than somewhere to park a deckchair. The 'urban homestead' movement is on the rise, with the blogosphere rapidly filling up with city farmers keen to share their expertise on salads and compost-making. The East and West Coasts of the USA are leading the charge, though cities such as London, Berlin and Amsterdam are close behind. It's a modern take on rural homesteading, when hard-working settlers tilled the soil and tended animals because they had to. These days, of course, no one living in a First World city has to keep hens to eat eggs or grow broccoli to fill their stomachs. And yet more and more of us are turning our back gardens over to fruit and vegetables and taking pleasure in tapping back into a more self-sufficient age.

These urban homesteaders might treat their gardens like a farm, but they have no intention of moving to the countryside. Novella Carpenter's book, *Farm City,* tells of her inner-city homestead in Oakland, San Francisco and her nightly dumpster searches for food to feed her backyard pigs. 'Someday I might move to the country,' she says. 'But while I'm young and into leading a city life, complete with movie theatres, museums, restaurants, public transportation, I'm happy right here.'

There's nothing new about city people wanting to get their hands in the soil. In the 1970s a wave of idealists left US cities to set up communities and 'go back to the land'. The difference is that this time, the urbanites are staying put. 'Urban homesteader' Kelly Coyne lives in the heart of Los Angeles where her twelfth-of-an-acre garden (a little larger than a tennis court) keeps her and her partner Erick almost self-sufficient in fruit and vegetables. 'We don't wish to retreat to the countryside and live like hermits in a plywood shack. We believe people

are best off living in cities and cooperating with other like-minded folks. We relate this movement to a time when people enjoyed the conveniences of city life but were also somewhat self-reliant, too,' she says. 'All in all, it's a form of idealism which is more integrated and grounded than the escapist fantasies of the 1970s. There's less nudity, too.'

In Brooklyn, New York, the urban homesteading heartland, wannabe henkeepers and apartment-farmers can buy seed and take classes in vermicomposting at 'pop-up' shop Hayseed's Big City Farm Supply. Round here, beards are, apparently, de rigeur. Christian Lander, creator of the satirical blog Stuff White People Like, told the *New York Post*, 'Last time I was in Brooklyn, it looked like every guy there was about to ship out for the Civil War'. As Brooklyn resident Marie Viljoen puts it, 'I joke that you're not allowed to live here unless you have a cow on your roof'.

We're all growing food for different reasons. Some do it to save money, others just to enjoy the taste of genuinely fresh tomatoes or strawberries. For some it's political, signalling a switch from a consumer- to a producer-lifestyle. But, whether you go the whole hog and invite bees and hens to join your urban veg patch or just stick to the crops, it's a lot of fun. You'll eat delicious food every day, feel better connected to nature and the seasons, and you'll find a quiet sanctuary from the screech of the city. Beards are not compulsory.

TURN YOUR GARDEN INTO AN URBAN HOMESTEAD

First, decide on where the growing area will be, making sure you leave space for a compost bin and/or a wormery and somewhere to sit. When choosing your growing site, bear in mind that fruit and vegetables generally prefer lots of sunshine and a sheltered spot out of direct winds. Avoid sites too near trees or hedges if you can since the soil here will not only be shaded, but too dry.

raised beds or on the level?

Anyone who started growing food in the past 10 years would be forgiven for thinking fruit and vegetables will only grow in a raised bed. Dotting the world's allotments and gardens, these low wooden frames have their benefits – allowing you to grow on hardstanding, polluted or poorly drained ground – but they are not essential. Unless you are gardening on concrete, heavy clay soil, a former industrial site or on builders' rubble don't write off growing directly into garden soil. They've been doing it for centuries.

how to prepare garden soil for growing fruit and vegetables

Fruit and vegetables take a lot out of the soil, so you need to make sure it's fertile. City garden soil, particularly in new developments, can be a surprisingly dingy thing, a thin top layer of fertile stuff over a repository of discarded builders' rubble. This project will show you what you've got.

how to prepare your soil for planting

Dig over the growing area with a garden fork, removing weeds and stones and breaking up clods of soil with the back of the fork. Add grit if necessary (see right). Then spread a layer (at least 15cm deep) of garden compost or well-rotted farmyard manure over the surface, loosely digging it into the soil. If you don't have your own garden compost yet, try contacting your city waste department – they often sell green waste quite cheaply.

how to FIND OUT WHAT TYPE OF SOIL YOU HAVE

you will need

A handful of garden soil

5 minutes

how to do it

Pick up a small handful of soil, squeeze it and try to form it into a ball shape between your palms. Then rub the soil between your fingers, noting what it feels like.

If your soil won't form a ball and feels gritty, it's a sandy soil. If it forms a sticky ball that retains its shape, then it's a clay or silty soil. A clay soil can also be formed into a rope shape if you rub it between your hands. A loamy soil will make a ball but it will crumble easily when you squeeze it.

Each soil has different benefits and drawbacks. If your soil is sandy, it will be easy to dig, drain well and heat up quickly in the spring. But it will also lose nutrients and water fast – so add lots of compost to it. Silty soils hold moisture well but also benefit from adding compost. Clay soils are heavy and can waterlog easily, but if you stay off them when wet and dig in lots of compost and some horticultural grit (a couple of shovelfuls per square metre) they can become very fertile. Loam is a winning combination of all the soils above, combining good drainage with an ability to hold on to nutrients. Keep it in good shape by adding a mulch of compost every year.

tip When you harvest a plant, get into the habit of mulching the soil around it with garden compost. Crops take up a lot of nutrients as they grow and a mulch restores the fertility of the soil.

COMPOST, MANURE OR WORMS?

If you're lucky enough to live near a city farm you have a great source of farmyard manure. Make sure it's well rotted – ideally three years old and with no smell – or it could burn your plants.

For most us, though, homemade garden compost is the way to a fertile soil and to healthy fruit and vegetables. Put the stuff on your garden and it improves drainage and suppresses weed growth. It also retains moisture in the soil, so cutting down on watering, and it feeds the plants, making everything grow bigger and better. Making your own compost for your crops from kitchen scraps and plant waste is vital since you will return nutrients to the soil rather than throw them in the bin. If you make it properly, compost won't even smell.

where to put your compost bin

However magical the process of composting might be, you're unlikely to find the compost bin itself an object of beauty, so you'll probably want to site it in an inconspicuous place. Leave some room around it so that you can turn the heap, and – although it shouldn't really smell if you add the right stuff – you might not want to site it right next to your outdoor dining table. A shady, out-of-the-way corner is ideal, leaving the sunny areas of the garden for growing crops or for sitting in a deckchair.

what to compost?

The secret of composting is to combine green stuff (such as soft plant material and kitchen scraps) with brown stuff (twigs and cardboard). You want to aim for a bit more 'brown' than 'green' – but we all have so much cardboard to recycle these days that there's no problem finding 'brown'. Add raw fruit and vegetable scraps, tea bags and coffee grounds, but don't add dairy, meat or fish products, and only add lawn clippings in small quantities or the heap will turn to green mush. Chop up woody prunings or they'll still be there in years to come. Annual weeds are okay to add, but any perennial weeds should be binned or soaked in a bucket of water with a lid for at least two weeks before adding to the compost. Otherwise they'll appear in your compost next year.

Turn your compost bin every couple of months with a garden fork, adding a bit of water if it's too dry and adding more 'brown' stuff if it gets slimy. Once the compost no longer smells like rotting food and has the consistency of moist chocolate cake (usually about six months, but longer over winter), it's ready to spread on your garden. A 10cm layer in autumn is ideal. Just leave it there and let the worms take it down into the soil.

how to MAKE A COMPOST BIN FOR FREE (OR AT LEAST, FOR VERY LITTLE)

Many cities provide free compost bins, though they are often plastic and therefore not the prettiest. You can make your own, more natural-looking compost bin from wooden pallets – especially if you're prepared to forage for them at the back of shops, building sites and in skips. It's worth asking permission before taking any pallets, since some are returned to the supplier for a deposit.

you will need

4 wooden pallets of roughly the same size

8 plastic cable ties, the longest you can find

45 minutes

when to do it

Any time of year

how to do it

Stand the pallets upright to form a square, then tie the corners together with the cable ties.

If you want to make an adjoining compost bin at a later date – even a small garden will soon produce enough to fill one bin – you just need to find three more pallets and attach them to the one you've already made.

When you want to turn the compost or empty the bin, simply cut through the cable ties either side of the front pallet, so that it falls forward letting you access the compost easily. Then use new cable ties to reattach the pallet afterwards.

LEFT: Beehive compost bins blend attractively into the garden setting and prevent the compost area from turning into an eyesore.

ABOVE: Tap off the brown liquid that the worms produce and use it diluted as a useful plant feed.

RIGHT: mix a couple of handfuls of worm compost into tired containers for an instant boost.

be a worm farmer

A compost bin is not for you if you have a patio garden, balcony or roof garden since you need soil on to which to place a compost bin. A wormery, however, is ideal. Taking up less space than a compost bin, this ingenious system uses brandling worms to digest kitchen scraps, turning them into super-fertile worm casts that make great soil conditioner. Mix a couple of handfuls into tired compost in containers and you'll give it an instant boost; or dig it thoroughly into garden soil. (Don't just leave it on the soil surface or it will dry rock hard.) A wormery produces compost about four times a year, and the brown liquid that can be tapped off at the bottom makes a great plant food when diluted one part to ten.

what do worms eat?

You can maintain a healthy diet for the worms by adding a 50:50 mixture of kitchen waste (or garden prunings) and cardboard. The key is little and often: a sudden deluge will overwhelm the worms and won't be eaten – resulting in smelly rotting food. Some people give their worms cooked vegetables and pasta, bread, cheese or pizza – and they can digest these in moderation – but it's easy to add too much, so it's best to start with raw fruit and vegetables until you get to know your worms better.

when to 'harvest' the worm compost?

Most wormeries are simply a rotating system of stacked plastic trays with perforated bases so the worms can make their way freely from one tray to another. You put new scraps in the top tray and, as it becomes full, take the bottom tray out, empty the compost out, and pop the now-empty tray on the top. When it's ready, after about four months, worm compost is brown, moist and spongy, with no discernible smell.

There will probably still be some worms living in this compost. You can add them to the garden where they will do no harm, but if you don't want your wormery to lose too many of its useful inhabitants you'll have to separate them out first. You can do this by hand, but it's a slow, wriggly job. It's easiest to just put the full tray on the top of the wormery and leave it, with the lid off, for about half an hour. The worms will wriggle away from the light and burrow down into the compost and through the holes at the bottom of the tray. You can then scoop off the top few worm-free centimetres of compost with a trowel. Then leave for another half an hour to let the worms wriggle down further and repeat until the tray is empty.

In city gardens, space is always an issue so it's best to grow crops that really deliver. Some of the following suggestions will keep cropping for months on end, making a real impression on your supper. Others taste so good fresh that growing them yourself is a must. All of the following crops will grow well in the space-challenged conditions of the urban jungle.

5 perfectly ripe crops

Grow these crops yourself and you can pick them at the perfect moment – the point of ripeness when the flavours and juiciness are at their peak. No more of those hard-as-golf ball peaches or acidic strawberries, picked early by the supermarkets to make it easy to get them to store. Spoil yourself with the tastes of these five and you will never want to buy supermarket versions again.

Raspberries

With their bristly stems and workmanlike flowers these might not be pretty plants, but raspberries are generous, each cane giving punnets of velvety berries that are expensive in the shops. Bees love the flowers too, and, of course, the fruit makes fantastic jam. When properly ripe, raspberries are squishy in the extreme and don't last long so shops tend to sell them firm, underripe and sour. If you're lucky enough to find a punnet of ripe ones for sale, chances are the bottom layer will already be mouldy. Grow raspberries yourself and you can pick, squish and eat them at their finest.

Autumn-fruiting varieties, such as Autumn Bliss or Caroline are the least effort, requiring no supports and a single cut right to the ground every February. Summer-fruiting varieties such as Malling Jewel and Glen Ample need to be supported with horizontal wires strung between two strong posts or attached to a fence or wall. Cut the fruited canes to the ground once you have finished harvesting them. The canes that haven't fruited yet should be left and tied in to the wires since they will produce fruit the following summer.

Buy bare canes in autumn or winter or container-grown plants in the spring and plant about 40cm apart in free-draining soil. Bare canes should be planted at the same depth they were in the nursery – they will have a visible soil mark on them so it's easy to get this right – and cut down to about 30cm after planting. Raspberries don't like soggy roots, but they do need to be kept moist so add lots of organic matter to the soil before planting, water well after planting and mulch the rows with compost every spring to stop the shallow roots from drying out. Raspberries don't like to be confined to a pot, so this is one to plant direct into the ground. If growing summer varieties, get your supports in place before you plant, making sure your parallel wires and posts are strong enough to support the fully grown canes. Birds with their beady eyes on your berries can be deterred with netting if necessary.

Strawberries

Long-lasting, prolific, low-maintenance, pretty and as happy in a hanging basket as it is in regimented rows in a garden bed… is the strawberry the perfect urban crop? Supermarket strawberries can be little more than anaemic-fleshed bullets, so acidic they make your mouth screw up, particularly, of course, when you buy them out of season. But grow them yourself and you can pick them when they actually smell and taste of strawberry and don't need any sugar to make them edible.

As shallow-rooted plants, strawberries are incredibly versatile, happy in grow bags and hanging baskets. Planted in the ground, they will fruit for several years before becoming exhausted, by which time you will have had plenty of opportunities to peg down the 'runners', baby plants that grow off the parent plant on long stems, into the soil to make new ones.

Strawberries will be sweetest in a sunny spot though will tolerate partial shade. To grow them you can either buy spidery-looking bare-rooted plants in the autumn or spring for a summer crop or buy potted plants throughout the spring and summer. These will give you only a small crop the first year so the bare-rooted plants are probably preferable.

For small spaces, an everbearing variety such as the sweet and aromatic Mara de Bois is a good choice since you get two harvests a year, one in early summer, the next in early autumn. Or choose a range of varieties that fruit at different times so you can have a long-term strawberry supply. Cambridge Favourite, Gariguette, Chelsea Pensioner and Florence are all delicious and will provide you with ripe strawberries from early to late summer.

Plant in well-cultivated soil, preferably to which garden compost or well-rotted manure has been added. Space plants about 30cm apart in holes large enough to allow their spidery roots to spread out comfortably, and set the crown of the plant (the pointy bit at the centre) so that it sits on the surface of the soil – this avoids the plant either drying out or rotting. Water well and then feed every fortnight with a high-potash fertiliser such as liquid seaweed or a tomato feed and harvest when the fruits look too good to resist. A good rule of thumb, taste-wise, is to wait until a fruit turns perfectly red and then wait one more day before picking.

At the end of the season, snip the old browning leaves to within 10cm of the crown (apart from 'ever-bearing' varieties which can be left as they are). It's a good idea to mulch in early spring with garden compost.

Slugs and snails can be a pest so a sprinkling of organic slug pellets is worth trying. Biting into a strawberry only to find a small slug curled up inside is something you don't want to do more than once.

• See page 73 for tips on growing strawberries in containers

'Eating a tomato, viney and sweet and still warm off the plant, is an experience not to be sniffed at.'

Tomatoes

Eating a tomato, viney and sweet and still warm off the plant is an experience not to be sniffed at. Try sweet, yellow Sungold, old favourite Gardener's Delight, mini plums Rosada or Red Pear or crunchy, dusky skinned Black Krim. Or if you can guarantee a long, hot summer try a beefsteak variety such as Costuluto Fiorentino or big heritage American varieties such as Brandywine, perfect for making sauces to preserve your urban harvest.

Sow tomato seeds, barely covered by a layer of compost, in small pots inside in mid spring, then transplant them outside in early summer in a sunny, sheltered spot in well-cultivated soil that has had lots of manure or garden compost added. Tomatoes are hungry plants so feed every fortnight with a high-potash feed and keep them well watered. If growing cordon or tall varieties, it's a good idea to pinch out the sideshoots that form between the stem and leaves to channel the plant's energy into fruit production.

Generally untroubled by slugs and snails, tomatoes do occasionally suffer from blight, a fungal disease that turns the leaves brown and renders the fruit inedible. If you are unlucky enough to be struck with this, pick the fruit immediately even if it isn't ripe – green tomato chutney is better than no tomatoes at all.

• See page 73 for tips on growing tomatoes in containers, page 66 for How to Save Your Own Tomato Seed

Plums

A Victoria plum tree laden with fruit is one of the most delicious sights of summer. It's not easy to buy ripe plums because they are squishy and don't keep well, so they're perfect for garden growing. Most plum trees are so accommodating that you'll have fruit left over for gorgeous jam. For small gardens, choose a tree on a dwarfing rootstock such as Pixie (which will keep the tree from growing taller than 6 foot), and either plant direct in the soil or in a pot at least 45cm in diameter. Plums love the sun but will crop well even in shade. No pruning is required for a decent crop, though pruning to shape the tree must be done in spring or summer to avoid the fungal disease silver leaf. While trees planted in the ground don't generally need feeding, potted trees would benefit from a fortnightly high-phosphate feed once they have set fruit – liquid

seaweed feed works well. Varieties-wise, you can't go much better than the classic rosy-skinned Victoria, though the green Cambridge Gage is delicious too.

• See page 73 for tips on growing plums in containers

Peaches and apricots

Most shop-bought peaches and apricots taste like cotton wool wrapped in chamois leather: grow them yourself and they're simply ambrosial, with meltingly soft flesh. Peregrine and Avalon Pride are good peach varieties and you can't go wrong with apricot Tomcot. Grow them in a fan shape against a south-facing fence or wall, or try a dwarf variety in a pot (of at least 45cm in diameter) and you can guarantee the sweetest crops. Feed them as you would plums (see above) and avoid pruning in winter to prevent fungal disease. Fan-trained peaches and apricots will crop better if pruned correctly. It is best to buy from a specialist supplier who can provide pruning instructions.

• See also blueberries and figs (page 73)

5 straight-into-the-pot crops

If any group of crops really proves the benefit of picking and throwing into the cooking pot within minutes, these do. Whether you eat them raw or cook these crisp, sweet vegetables before the natural sugars can turn to starch, you will really taste the difference.

Sweetcorn

They make tall plants as high as 2 metres, take up a lot of room, and each plant will produce only a couple of cobs, but if you can spare the space for sweetcorn, you really won't regret it. Store-bought sweetcorn is often past its best, the kernels slimy and starchy. Show-off home growers have the water on to boil even before they twist a ripe cob from the plant, such is the tender sweetness of really fresh sweetcorn. Go for a Tendersweet variety such as Swift or Lark and you will get sweet, soft cobs even in a cool climate.

You can buy sweetcorn as plants, but it's easy to start it off from seed on a windowsill inside or a greenhouse in mid spring. Push two seeds just below the surface of the compost in a 7.5cm pot. Remove the weaker seedlings when they have germinated. When the roots start to come out of the bottom of the pot transplant each seedling to a sunny spot in the garden in soil that has had plenty of garden compost or well-rotted manure dug in. Plant your seedlings 45cm apart in a block formation. This is necessary to ensure you get a decent fill of kernels since sweetcorn is wind-pollinated – the male flowers at the top drop pollen on to the female tassels below.

As the plants grow watch for slugs and snails and support the plant with a cane if necessary. Mulching the base or piling up soil around the bottom of the stem also helps with stability. Water well, especially when flowering, and feed fortnightly with a liquid seaweed feed or wormery tea when the cobs start to swell. When the tassels turn chocolate brown in late summer, your cobs are ready to investigate. Press a fingernail into a kernel; if the juice is watery it is not yet ripe; if it's paste-like, it's past its best; if it's milky, it is ready for the pot.

tip If space is tight in your garden, try underplanting your sweetcorn with salad crops or dwarf beans.

Carrots

Go for early varieties such as Amsterdam Forcing or Early Nantes, which taste particularly sweet just after harvesting. You can harvest finger-sized carrots from about eight weeks, which are delicious briefly steamed whole or eaten raw. If you sow every three weeks, you should have a constant supply.

Sow carrots direct into the ground in a sunny spot from early spring, in rows or patches, thinning plants to about 5cm apart. They don't like a particularly fertile soil so there's no need to add organic matter, but do make sure you remove any stones, since these can cause the carrots to fork.

Keep seedlings well watered and watch out for slugs and snails, which can decimate a row of seedlings overnight – organic slug pellets are handy here. Carrot fly can also be a pest since their maggots tunnel into the roots. The telltale sign is reddish leaves that wilt in hot weather. You can dispense with this problem by growing your carrots under horticultural fleece or in a raised bed at least 60cm high – the flies don't fly that high. Sowing thinly also helps since if you thin seedlings later the smell can attract flies.

Sugarsnap and mangetout peas

Another sweet contender, sugarsnap and mangetout peas are much better in a small garden than regular podded types since you get a lot more pea for your plant. Sugarsnaps Sugar Bon or Sugar Ann and mangetouts Norli or purple Shiraz guarantee crisp sweetness by the podful whether steamed or crunched raw. Sow direct in the soil in late spring in wide, shallow trenches about 5cm deep and 15cm wide, spacing your seeds roughly 5cm apart. Sowing in the pattern of five spots on a die works well. Cover with soil and firm in. Push twiggy sticks into the ground or provide trellis or netting they can cling to. Peas are happy in sun or partial shade and don't need particularly fertile soil to grow well, but they do require good drainage, so add organic matter if you have a heavy soil. Water well after flowering to ensure crunchy pods, which are best picked when they're about as long as your finger.

Asparagus

Although not ideal for a small garden, asparagus is a must if you have a spare 10 metres. Picking your own crop in late spring feels like a trip to your own luxury food hall, the freshly picked spears so crisp and sweet you can eat them raw (although let's not kid ourselves that they don't taste better cooked and smothered in mayonnaise or melted butter). Gijnlim and Connover's Colossal are good varieties. Plant the spidery 'crowns' (as baby plants are known) in the spring in thoroughly weeded soil. Dig a trench 30cm wide and 20cm deep, add some compost or well-rotted manure and then pile up a 10cm-high central ridge of excavated soil down the trench on to which the crowns can sit, their roots spread out either side. Backfill the trench with soil and compost. After an initial watering, asparagus can be watered fairly sparingly since it is pretty drought resistant. Leave 45cm between trenches. It's also fairly resistant to pests, though the black and yellow asparagus beetle may put in an appearance. Squishing the beetles by hand is the best defence.

Asparagus is not a fast food crop. You won't be able to harvest during the following year, and only sparingly the next, but after that you can harvest your heart out. And it's worth the wait. Honest.

Broad beans

Grow these beans yourself and you can eat them small and sweet – when they're no bigger than your thumbnail – utterly delicious steamed briefly and eaten unskinned in a warm salad of baby new potatoes, beetroot, feta and mint. For a bonus crop that tastes like spinach, nip off the top few centimetres of the bean plant, steam and serve with plenty of butter and black pepper. This early harvest also avoids the problem of blackfly that tend to cluster around the growing tips.

Choose the Crimson Flowered variety broad beans and you will also get delightful dark pink scented flowers, as pretty as any ornamental flower. Sow beans in the ground in early spring about 5cm deep and 20cm apart. If you sow them in double rows it's easy to support them with bamboo canes and parallel rows of string. Some varieties such as Aquadulce Claudia can be sown in autumn to get ahead of the game and tend to appeal less to blackfly.

5 constant croppers

Some fruit and vegetable crops have one magnificent hurrah ... and then nothing. Others chug on reliably in the background, providing a constant supply of leaves, fruit and stems for months at a time.

For the urban homesteader, these are invaluable. Include these in your edible garden and you will always have something to harvest.

Lettuce and other salad crops

All salad leaves are prolific and when you grow them yourself you not only enjoy when they're so fresh they almost squeak, but also get a really vibrant, interesting mix, from **baby spinach** to **pea shoots** and **sorrel**.

Salad crops can be sown from early spring – started off indoors in small pots – right through to early autumn. If you sow a hardy variety such as **Winter Density** or **Four Seasons** at this time and protect it over the winter with a couple of layers of fleece it will give you a very welcome spring crop.

Regular salad sowings every two or three weeks should give you a constant crop of leaves even in a small garden. Most salads like a moist soil but don't require additional feeding. A site where compost has been added the previous season is ideal. All lettuces and salads run to flower eventually, turning the leaves bitter, but you can avoid this happening too quickly by keeping all salads well watered. A partially shady position in summer can also help – otherwise give salads a sunny spot.

Lettuce can be sown thickly for baby leaves – these can be cut and will re-sprout once or twice before needing to be replaced – but you will get much more lettuce if you thin the seedlings 30cm apart and let them grow to maturity. That way you can take the outer leaves, leaving the inner ones to keep growing. One lettuce can crop for at least a month if you treat it like this. There is a plethora of lettuce varieties to choose from – frilly loose-leaf types such as **Oakleaf, Red and Green Salad Bowl, Black Seeded Simpson** or **Red Sails** are great, as are crunchy **Cos** or **Romaine** types such as **Lobjoits** or **Crisp Mint**, which are just perfect for Caesar salads.

But salad isn't confined to lettuce. Try sowing a few rows of peas – marrowfat dried peas from a food store will do fine – to harvest as crunchy pea shoots. Sow about 2cm deep so thickly they are almost touching and snip off the top few centimetres when they are about 10cm tall.

There are plenty of ready-mixed salad seed packets you can buy that give you a good variety of textures and flavours, or you can build up your own mix. Tangy, lemony leaf **Buckler's leaf sorrel** will pep up your salads. Sow in rows in partial shade and thin to about 10cm apart, snipping leaves when young. For something colourful, try **Beetroot Bull's Blood** for sweet purple leaves. Sown about 5cm apart, you can snip the young leaves repeatedly. **Chard** and **spinach** sown 5cm apart will give you tender, sweet baby leaves while winter purslane provides a succulent crunch.

Sow a row or two of mild tasting **lamb's lettuce** or **mâche** from mid spring to late summer, thinned to about 15cm apart (hardy enough to last through winter if given some fleece protection) and your garden will provide a delicious salad mix.

Kai lan

With a taste somewhere between pak choi and purple sprouting broccoli, and a winning habit of producing a seemingly endless supply of shoots, leaves, stems and flowers – all of which are edible – this Asian green is a bit of an urban grower's sensation. Sow it in mid-spring in modules or little pots inside and transplant when the plants have five leaves into a sunny or partially shaded spot, spaced about 30cm apart. Keep it well watered and it will grow up to 45cm, cropping all summer until the first frosts. If you snip off a shoot, it will just grow another. Try it stir-fried or steamed and you will be converted.

Runner and French beans

These vigorous climbers will scale trellises or wigwams easily, providing you with succulent beans from mid summer right into autumn. Runner beans, in particular, also look very pretty on the plot with their scarlet flowers. Sow runner or French beans direct in a sunny or partially shaded spot, ideally in soil that has had compost or well-rotted manure added the previous year. Sow seeds 5cm deep and 10cm apart and give them something to twine up such as a bamboo cane.

Pick runner beans before they get stringy (anything longer than 12cm is unlikely to be good), de-string and cut them finely then steam for a few minutes and there is no vegetable more summery. Scarlet Emperor, Enorma or Painted Lady will all do well. French beans are tender enough to be eaten whole. Climbing versions are very productive and come in yellow (Rocquencourt), purple (Violette) or green (Cobra, Blue Lake).

Globe artichokes

They may take up quite a lot of your precious growing area, growing up to 1.5m tall and 1m wide, but do consider including a couple of these silvery beauties. The plants are statuesque, drought-tolerant and, when mature, will each produce about 12 artichokes a year, often more. Pick and throw them straight into boiling water to really benefit from the sweetness they have when fresh.

After about five years the plants will get tired but helpfully, by then, they'll have produced baby plants at the base that you can cut off and re-plant elsewhere in spring. Green Globe produces classic, large heads while Violetta di Chioggia has very pretty purple ones. Buy as plants and space them at least a metre apart in garden soil in a sunny spot in spring. Add grit if you have a heavy soil and dig in some garden compost. Due to their size, the back of a sunny border is ideal. Once plants have established, you should only need to water them sparingly. Mulch in early spring with garden compost. Hard as it might be to resist, try not to pick artichokes in their first summer to allow them a chance to establish.

Nasturtiums

These sprawling flowers are troopers, covering bare patches of soil, and blooming their hearts out with retina-burning orange and yellow flowers. They feed us too: the leaves can be chopped into mashed potatoes making a spicy colcannon; the flowers bring a peppery hit to salads (and don't look bad either); and the seedpods make wonderful crunchy pickles.

Sow nasturtiums in spring, choosing a bush or trailing variety depending on whether you want a compact look or a sprawling jungle. Empress of India nasturtiums will grow in pretty much any soil and any location, though a dry, thin soil in full sun is their favourite place. Sow a trailing variety by a wall and watch it scramble up it. Once you have grown nasturtiums they freely self-seed so you won't have to re-sow them.

• See also chard (page 25), kale (page 25), salads (page 56–57), and herbs (page 34–36).

how to MAKE A JAR OF NASTURTIUM PICKLES

Pickles are a great way to preserve the produce of a small garden since a little goes a long way. Nasturtium pickles add a sweet-peppery crunch to potato salads or cheese and ham sandwiches.

you will need

2 handfuls of green nasturtium seedpods

1 teaspoon salt

3 sprigs of tarragon

6 peppercorns

2 peeled garlic cloves (optional)

100ml white wine or cider vinegar

A sterilised jar

when to do it

Mid summer to early autumn

how to do it

Put the seedpods in 150ml of water and add the salt. Leave for 24 hours. Drain the seedpods and put in the jar along with the tarragon sprigs, peppercorns and, if you're using them, garlic cloves. Fill almost to the top with vinegar, covering the seedpods. tarragon sprigs, peppercorn and garlic cloves by at least 1 cm. Seal. Put in the fridge and eat within a year.

how to PLANT AN EDIBLE HEDGE

Instead of immediately planting a climber to hide your boring fence, consider an edible hedge. Plant one of these and not only will it bring a bit of the native countryside into the city, blossom beautifully in spring and encourage wildlife, but it will vastly increase your urban harvest, giving you plenty of fruit and berries for jams and jellies.

All of the plants listed will work in an edible hedge. Either plant the suggested combination or mix and match as you like. You could have a whole hedge of one plant, but the more varieties you cram in, the more natural the hedge will look. Two metres is probably the minimum length for a reasonable edible hedge, and if you have room for a longer one, adjust the quantities of plants accordingly. You could also add other edible hedging plants such as blackthorn (*Prunus spinosa*) for sloe gin, or cornelian cherry (*Cornus mas*). Even raspberries will be happy growing up through an edible hedge. Choose bareroot plants around 60-90cm tall for a fast establishing hedge.

you will need

A planting area at least 2m long and 1m wide (adjust plant quantities if larger)

A bareroot blackberry (*Rubus fruticosus*)

A bareroot hazel (*Corylus avellana*)

A bareroot field rose (*Rosa arvensis*)

A bareroot cherry plum (*Prunus cerasifera*) or Myrobalan plum

A bareroot wild pear (*Pyrus communis*)

A bareroot crab apple (*Malus sylvestris*)

Garden fork

Garden spade

Large bucket

Garden compost to enrich the ground

2 hours

when to do it
Autumn to early spring

how to do it
Place your bareroot plants in the bucket of water. Dig over the soil thoroughly, removing any weeds and then fork in about one bucketful of garden compost per plant. Push your spade into the ground to make a slit to plant into, moving the spade back and forth to make a small crevice. Make a crevice for each plant at 33cm intervals along the line of the hedge and pop each bareroot plant in to its original planting depth (look for the tell-tale line on the stem). Firm the soil back in around the plant with your heels. Water well and continue to keep it well watered and weed-free for at least a year as the hedge establishes.

what next?
Keep your edible hedge in shape by trimming it lightly every year once all the fruits have been harvested in late autumn. Cut the old, fruited blackberry canes down to the base.

This is an urban forager's paradise, not only giving you hazelnuts, blackberries and sweet plums the size of cherries, but also providing you with hips for rosehip syrup (see page 127) and crab apples for jelly (see page 125).

save your seeds

It's easy to grow crops and flowers from seed you've saved the previous autumn. You'll save money and it's extremely satisfying to see your seeds germinate after a winter in a Clip-Lock box. It also gives you the opportunity to save seed from plants that have performed best in your conditions – the biggest, tastiest sweet pepper plants, the most vigorous tomatoes. The next generation plant will then be much more suited to your local soil, growing conditions and weather than something from a shop-bought seed that came from thousands of miles away.

how to COLLECT AND SAVE SEED

you will need

Dry seeds or seedheads

Brown paper bags

Small envelopes (wage packets are ideal and easily found in stationers)

An airtight container such as a Clip-Lock box or Tupperware

A couple of sachets of silica gel crystals; these are easily bought online or save some next time you buy a new pair of shoes or a wallet

Pencil

Secateurs or scissors

when to do it
A dry day in late summer/early autumn

how to do it
Find a plant with ripe seeds. You will know this because the seed case will be brown and papery (see How Do I Know if Seed is Ready to Collect?, page 65) for more details). Pick the seedheads either by snapping them off or cutting them with your scissors and then pop them into the brown paper bag. Label the bag.

Lay the seeds out to dry on a greenhouse bench, warm windowsill or an airing cupboard. Let them lie loosely in open cardboard boxes or in open paper bags or on newspaper, making sure you keep them labelled. Don't use plastic bags because the seeds will sweat and rot.

After a week or so, when you are sure that the seeds are completely dry, remove any seed cases or chaff (which can encourage rotting) and put the seeds into small envelopes, making sure to label them clearly with the type of plant, where they were found and the date they were collected. Then put the envelopes in your airtight box along with a couple of sachets of silica gel. Store in a cool, dark place such as a drawer. The worst places to store seed are damp greenhouses or garden sheds. The following spring, sow as usual.

LEFT: Runner beans, teasels and chillies – seeds are generally ready to collect when the seed case or head is dry, brown and papery.

ABOVE RIGHT: Collect seed from rosehips when they are still red.

BELOW RIGHT: Allow seedheads of the globe thistle to dry fully before shaking them out into a paper bag.

Q: can I collect seed from any plant?

A: Yes, unless they are rare wild flowers (see Can I Collect Wildflower Seed?, page 136) or F1 hybrids. F1 hybrids are plants that have been specially bred to be vigorous and seed saved from them will not 'come true to type', ie plants may bear little resemblance to their parents. It's therefore not really worth saving seed from them because you don't know what you will get. It will always clearly say on a seed packet if a variety is an F1 hybrid or not. Many vegetable seeds in the shops are F1 hybrids because they produce vigorous, productive plants, sometimes with built-in disease and pest resistance.

Heritage or heirloom vegetable seeds tend not to be F1s so are great for saving at home. Knowing that you are preserving a little bit of the past adds to the pleasure. Heritage vegetables are becoming increasingly popular with home growers drawn to their sense of history, and often curious names – Fat Lazy Blonde lettuce anyone? They can look beautiful too – a patch of crimson flowered broad beans gives foxgloves a run for their money (and you can't eat foxgloves).

Q: how do I know if seed is ready to collect?

A: Generally, seed is ready if the seed, seed case or head is dry, brown and papery. Common annual and biennial flowers such as nigella, nicotiana, hollyhocks, foxgloves and poppies are crying out for their seed to be collected, their seedheads rattling when you shake them. Just put the head inside a paper bag and shake the seeds out.

Larger seeds, such as calendula, sunflowers or cosmia, are ready to harvest when they are brown and brittle, while nasturtiums can be picked green and stored in a dry place for a couple of weeks until they turn brown. With pods such as runner beans or peas the seeds are ripe when the pod turns brown and wrinkly and the seeds inside are so hard that biting them with your teeth wouldn't leave an indentation. Some seed, such as that of tomatoes, requires a more specialist approach, see page 66.

10

EASY GARDEN FLOWER SEEDS TO COLLECT

If you are a seed-collecting beginner, these common garden flowers are a good place to start. See page 63 for collecting instructions.

Sweetpeas
Nigella
Nicotiana
Foxgloves
Marigolds
Hollyhocks
Honesty
Nasturtium
Sunflowers
Cosmia

10

EASY VEGETABLE SEEDS TO COLLECT

Runner, broad and French
   beans
Peas
Lettuce
Sweet pepper and chillis
Rocket (arugula)
Coriander
Radish
Cucumber
Basil
Parsley

how to SAVE YOUR OWN TOMATO SEED

If you have grown a particularly delicious tomato, why not repeat the experience next year by saving some seed? As long as the variety isn't an F1 hybrid (see page 65), it's well worth doing, particularly since tomato seed is not that cheap to buy.

could I just use a supermarket tomato?
You could save seed from a bought tomato, but it's not recommended unless you know for sure that the variety isn't an F1 hybrid and that it is suitable for growing in your climate.

you will need

A ripe, tasty, homegrown tomato that is not an F1 hybrid variety

A knife

A spoon

A bowl

A sieve

A plate

About 10 days

when to do it

Mid summer to early autumn

how to do it
Cut the tomato in half and scoop out the seed. Put it in a bowl, add water and leave in a warm place, giving the mixture a swirl a couple of times a day. After about three days, a pad of mould will form on the surface – throw this away and refill the container. Leave for three more days, during which any viable seed will sink to the bottom. Pour off the pulp and liquid then strain the seed in a sieve, rinse and leave to dry on a plate (not kitchen paper, since it will stick to it) for a couple of days before storing. The following spring, sow as usual.

tip Chuck any snails you find in the kitchen bin (they will crawl out of the compost). Organic slug pellets will deal with a slug problem. Nematodes are also very effective.

tip Don't forget the flowers! Every urban homestead needs beautiful blooms – and they'll bring in the bees. Sweet peas, cosmos, nigella, sunflowers and nasturtiums are a good place to start.

RURBANITE: Megan Paska the urban homesteader, Brooklyn, New York

Thirty-year-old Megan doesn't just grow vegetables in the backyard of her rented Brooklyn apartment building: she keeps hens too. And bees on the roof. One of a growing band of hipster rurbanites in New York, Megan is a proud exponent of the pleasures urban homesteading can bring, spreading the word through blogging, tweeting and teaching courses on bees, hens and vegetable growing.

For Megan the motivation to grow food is an attempt to take back some sense of control. 'I think modern people are interested in essential skills like growing food because it feels terrible to be so out of touch. We depend on faceless entities to do for us what we ought to be able to do for ourselves. The current state of our food system is an example of what kind of horrors can happen when we give corporations too much control over something as critical as food production. Beyond that, it's just really fun and rewarding

'People are interested in growing food because it feels terrible to be so out of touch.'

to eat the fruits of your own labour. It's an easy thing to fall in love with.'

Megan chooses to grow crops that are expensive to buy at farmers' market or taste better when harvested very fresh. Tomatoes, peppers and aubergines crowd the raised beds as well as greens such as chard, kale, lettuce and pea shoots. Radishes, cucumber and squash are other favourites and a herb garden adorns the roof of her chicken coop.

As Megan sees it, for intensely built-up cities such as New York, there has been a total disconnect from the natural food system. 'New York City couldn't sustain itself if we didn't have resources trucked in by the ton every hour,' she says. 'New Yorkers tend to feel isolated from the world of agriculture so I suppose our thriving food scene is an attempt at mimicking farm community in whatever way we can.'

be a container grower

If you have a small patio garden, a balcony or just a few windowsills, you can grow a surprising array of fresh food. As the world becomes more urbanised, more of us are living in apartments where balconies and rooftops offer exciting opportunities for growing your own. Architects are starting to take seriously the need to get our hands in the soil. Currently under construction in Milan, Italy is the Bosco Verticale, two apartment blocks that will be clothed in greenery, including 530 trees, 5,000 shrubs and 11,000 ground cover plants adding up to the equivalent of a hectare of forest. In Valencia, Spain, there are plans for a new apartment block that will feature balconies cantilevered 8m out from the side of the building, with growing pits deep enough to plant orange, lemon, olive and pine trees. It is called Torre Huerta, a nod to the 'huertas' or fruit and vegetable gardens that once skirted the city until absorbed into the urban sprawl.

Exciting as these projects are, you don't need to live in a specially adapted apartment block to grow fruit and vegetables in the city. Any balcony, roof terrace or patio garden can become a food-growing zone – providing you do it in containers. All the crops here grow particularly well in containers as long as you follow two basic rules. Use organic, peat-free multipurpose compost, and make sure the bottom of the container has drainage holes.

which pot to use?

You don't need to buy pots – you can create an entire vegetable garden from recycled containers, whether they're fruit cartons, plastic food tubs or old bread tins. Look under the stairs or in your kitchen cupboards – or ask at nearby food stores and delis for unwanted tins or crates. Wooden wine crates are sturdy and long-lasting, ply fruit crates less so, but fine for a quick crop. Cheap and cheerful are those bright rubber tubtrugs – perfect for larger crops – while plastic storage boxes from thrift stores are as cheap as chips. If the utilitarian look of clear plastic offends, you can disguise it with offcuts of reed, willow or bamboo screening picked up for a few pounds from garden centres.

how to MAKE A PLANTER FROM A JUICE CARTON

Cartons for milk or fruit juice are thrown away all the time – and the recycling systems of many countries are unable to process them – so why not turn them into planters? At the Prinzessinnengarten mobile community garden in Berlin (see page 31), the café gets through plenty of milk and juice cartons, so the garden has a ready supply to use for salad containers. These cartons make surprisingly robust growing pots because their waxed interior retains moisture well. They're also light and easy to carry. Salad crops (especially when harvested as cut-and-come-again crops), pea or sunflower shoots and herbs are particularly happy growing where your orange juice used to be.

what you need

A waxed cardboard juice or milk carton (with the lid screwed on)

A sharp, serrated kitchen knife or scissors

Organic, peat-free multipurpose compost

Suitable seed, such as salad, pea, herb or sunflower

15 minutes

when to do it

Any time of year

how to do it

Cut out two square panels on one side of the carton, leaving a central strip that can act as a carrying handle. Then make about six holes in the opposite side to let water drain away. Fill the carton with compost then sow your seed 2cm apart and cover with a thin layer of compost. Water well.

tip Think vertical: in tiny growing areas, lengths of plastic rain guttering (don't forget to make drainage holes) screwed into the wall make excellent containers for baby salad leaves, microgreens or pea and sunflower shoots and won't take up any of your ground space.

5 best crops for pots

Spring onions

These are useful container crops since they take up so little room but really make a mark on salads and Asian dishes or snipped over roast meats. Dot them between other crops, filling in the gaps between lettuce leaves. They will be ready for harvest after eight weeks and regular sowing from early spring to mid autumn will keep you in constant supply. Best grown in full sun or partial shade, though even shady sowings will crop. White Lisbon is a reliable variety.

Radishes

These bring a substantial crunch to any baby-leaf salad, but often fail to develop a root before running to flower. Radishes will grow well in a sunny pot, grow bag or window box at least 15cm deep, but don't overcrowd them – at least 7cm apart is best. Water well to keep them succulent, and harvest about a month after sowing to ensure they don't get woody. The long, white-tipped 'French Breakfast' is the prettiest variety, and 'Cherry Belle' is round perfection.

Chillies

There are three reasons to grow chillies in a small container garden: one, they like growing in a pot where their roots are snug and they can be moved into a scorching hot spot. Two, each plant is so prolific that just one pot is usually enough for all but the most capsaicin-inclined. And, three, when the peppers are red the plants look gorgeous. Sow inside in early spring on a sunny windowsill into small pots of compost, and then transplant outside into pots at least 20cm in diameter in late spring in the hottest position you can find. In autumn, bring your plants inside and you might be able to nudge them through winter into the next growing season. Excess chillies can be threaded together and hung up to dry. They look pretty in Christmas wreaths if craft is your thing.

The varieties of chilli available to grow is dizzying, ranging from the volcanic Habanero and Naga to the relatively mild Poblano. Some are yellow, some red, some pointy some stubby. All will bring a dash of colour and drama to a balcony, patio or windowsill.

PROJECT

STRING UP YOUR CHILLIES

Even one container chilli plant can provide a winter's worth of chillies if you dry them. Hang up your string of dried chillis somewhere in the kitchen for a vibrant reminder of your summer harvest and a ready supply to crush with a pestle and mortar.

you will need

Ripe chillies

Cotton thread

A needle

when to do it

Late summer to early autumn, when the chillies ripen

how to do it

Thread your needle and tie a knot in the thread. Push the needle through each chilli just below the hard green stem end, continuing until you have a thread of chillies. Wash your hands well afterwards and don't rub your eyes! Hang the chilli string up to dry in a warm, well-ventilated place.

Blueberries

Generous handfuls of sweet berries – firm, aromatic and without that horrible mushy texture of shop-bought ones – can be yours for very little effort in return. All that a blueberry bush asks of you is ericaceous or acidic compost (found in all garden centres), a fortnightly high-potash feed (such as tomato food or liquid seaweed), and a companion (two different varieties are best to ensure cross-pollination and plenty of fruit). Earliblue, Sunshine Blue and Bluecrop are all good varieties. No pruning is required apart from the removal of dead or crossing stems, and you get pretty spring flowers as a bonus.

Figs

Brown Turkey is the most popular variety, but Violetta and Brunswick are reliable too. They are ideal for planting in pots (at least 45cm in diameter) since they need their root growth to be restricted in order to set fruit properly. For this reason, if planting in the ground, choose a sunny spot and restrict the roots by making a pit about 60cm square lined with paving slabs or bricks. Either grow your tree as a freestanding bush or position your pot near a wall and prune it into a fan, attaching the long stems to parallel wires. Don't let your potted fig tree dry out and feed it from mid spring to late summer fortnightly with a liquid seaweed feed. Fruit should ripen by late summer; pick when squishy – any fruits that form after that should be removed since they won't ripen this side of winter – unless they are smaller than your little fingernail in which case they will be next summer's crop so should be left.

other good container crops

Kale – three plants per 30cm diameter pot. See also page 25.

Salad potatoes – place three first or second early potatoes on a 20cm layer of compost in a 30cm diameter pot or bag and add a further 30cm of compost. When the green shoots are about 20cm tall, add more compost to almost cover them. Keep earthing up the shoots until the pot is full. If growing in a bag, you can roll down the sides and unroll them as you add more compost. Once the plants start to flower, feed with a high-potash liquid or wormery tea (see page 46). Orla and Charlotte are good container varieties. Harvest as for soil-grown potatoes. See also page 26.

Chard – three plants per 30cm diameter pot. See also page 25.

New Zealand spinach – one plant per 30cm diameter pot. See also page 32.

Herbs – see pages 34–36.

Tomatoes – a grow bag or a 30cm diameter pot with a bamboo cane wigwam is ideal for three cordon plants, while bush varieties thrive in pots and large windowboxes. Hanging baskets are great for tumbling varieties such as Tumbling Tom. Don't let plants dry out and feed every fortnight with liquid seaweed or tomato food. See also page 51.

Strawberries – six plants per grow bag or three plants in a 30cm diameter hanging basket, pot or windowbox. See also page 48.

Carrots – sow seed about 5cm apart in 30cm diameter pots or large windowboxes at least 25cm deep. Mignon or Parmex are good container varieties. See page 54.

Plums – try a minarette Victoria or Cambridge Gage tree in a John Innes compost in a 45cm diameter pot. See also page 51.

Broad beans – five plants per 30cm diameter pot. See also page 54.

Lettuce and other salads – sow 5cm apart and grow as baby leaves or plant 20cm apart for mature heading lettuces in windowboxes or pots at least 15cm deep. See also pages 56–57.

Watercress – will thrive in a pot as long as the compost is kept damp. Sow thickly for the most generous crop and snip stems when you need them.

Sunflower shoots are nutty and crunchy, and can take only a week to go from seed to plate. Sow thickly and snip them before they form their second set of true leaves.

Dwarf French beans – see page 57 – 6-8 plants per 30cm diameter pot.

Kai lan – 3 plants per 30cm diameter pot.

tip All container-grown crops benefit from a fortnightly regular feed of liquid seaweed feed or diluted worm tea (see page 46).

how to MAKE GARDENING EQUIPMENT FOR FREE

When you're gardening on a small scale it seems silly to spend money on expensive equipment, especially if you can make it for free. It's recycling, too, so you're doing your environmental bit. Here are two options to consider after you've had your breakfast cereal.

you will need

A plastic pint milk jug with a handle

A craft knife or sharp scissors

PROJECT 1: MAKE A COMPOST SCOOP

Cut the bottom and part of the handle side off. Replace the lid and you have a robust scoop for getting compost into the small pots you need to start off seedlings.

PROJECT 2: MAKE A MINI CLOCHE

Cut the bottom of the jug off and push the bottle over vulnerable plants. On especially cold nights, replace the lid, otherwise leave the lid off so the plant can breathe. The cloche can also be used in the daytime to protect early-spring outside plantings from cold, wind, slugs and snails. Any clear plastic bottles – such as those for mineral water – can also be used to make a mini cloche.

tip You don't need to buy a propagator to protect germinating seedlings. Sow seed in recycled plastic fruit punnets and keep the lids to pop back on top. The holes in the lid allow air to circulate.

1

2

how to GROW MICROGREENS INSIDE

If you don't have any outside space at all – not even an exterior windowsill – you can still grow your own crops. Herbs and tomatoes will grow well inside, but easiest are microgreens. Any salad-leaf mix and many vegetable crops can be harvested at the 'micro' stage – just after the first pair of true leaves forms. Diminutive, but packing a punch above their weight in flavour, microgreens are a great crop for growing inside since they are eaten within 21 days of sowing.

you will need

Suitable seed, such as carrot, kale, fennel, pea, coriander, celery, basil, chard and beetroot

Multipurpose peat-free compost

A seed tray or plastic punnet (the ones in which fruit is sold are ideal)

A saucer or shallow tray

20 minutes

when to do it

All year round

how to do it

Make sure the punnet or tray has drainage holes and, if not, make some with a skewer or scissors. Put a 2cm layer of compost in the base. Then sow the seed on to the surface so it is almost touching. Small seed can be left uncovered but larger seed such as beetroot, chard, coriander and peas would benefit from a 0.25cm covering of compost. Fill the saucer with water and put the tray on it, then place in a light, warm spot. Add more water to the saucer when the surface of the compost dries out.

Harvest your plants with scissors when they have their first set of true leaves (though you can leave peas until they're about 10cm tall). Use these microgreens as a garnish or scattered into salads and sandwiches.

5 BEST MICROGREEN CROPS

Carrots
Fennel
Beetroot
Coriander
Basil

reclaim the street

Where does your territory end and public space begin? At the front door? At the end of the street? These are questions that city gardeners are starting to ask themselves. Let's face it, plants are rarely high on the priority list of city authorities, and much of our public planted space is underwhelming at best. A growing number of us have had enough of neglected flowerbeds, bare street planters and soulless roundabouts. So we're taking matters into our own hands, planting bulbs and throwing seed bombs.

Guerrilla gardeners fight the fight without permission. Others are on a more genteel road to urban prettification, planting their front gardens expressly for the benefit of the street. New York's Greenest Block in Brooklyn competition sees residents jostle for the most stunning streetfront displays, with exuberant pots cascading down brownstone steps and front gardens almost bursting through the fence.

The surreptitious thrill of planting without permission sparks people's imaginations. Artist Steve Wheen plants up holes in London streets with miniature gardens to 'put smiles on people's faces and alert them to potholes'. Based in Manchester, artist Paul Harfleet plants pansies at the site of homophobic attacks in cities. He photographs the site and puts the images on his website (thepansyproject.com), naming each photo after the abuse that was shouted at the victim. Another artist, Vanessa Harden, has developed the not entirely serious Precision Bombing Device 1, disguised as a camera lens, which allows the guerrilla user to shoot seed over urban fences. Acclaimed guerrilla Richard Reynolds (whose mantra is 'Let's fight the filth with forks and flowers!') harvests lavender from a central London roundabout, dries it and stuffs it into cushions. You could buy it in the upmarket store Liberty of London for a time.

Some cities have given up fighting guerrilla gardeners. In Vancouver, the authorities have allowed guerrilla gardeners to take over 250 public spaces. In Munich, you can now get a guerrilla gardening permit. However they choose to do it, though, one thing is certain; urbanites the world over are looking at public green spaces around their homes with a new sense of responsibility and pride.

And why not? With the smallest effort you can turn your street from a dull, sterile thoroughfare to a vibrant place to linger. As private gardens in cities become ever smaller and more precious, any plantable space outside the home is an opportunity to get out and get digging. And if the mass of tulips, sunflowers or cornfield meadow flowers you plant on the roadside makes a downtrodden commuter smile on their way to work, that's a bonus.

RURBANITE: Maina van der Zwan, guerrilla gardener, Amsterdam

Amsterdam is a city that knows how to garden. Plantable space in the city is precious and the residents are experts in making the most of every centimetre. A walk along the canal side in central Amsterdam turns up a treasure trove of joyful, creative urban gardening, with bike baskets planted with bulbs and climbing roses and lofty hollyhocks growing from what look like cracks in the pavement. Mini container gardens crowd every front step. It's no surprise that the city has a thriving guerrilla gardening scene.

Maina van der Zwan is one of those who has taken matters into his own hands. 'I've confiscated a piece of pavement in front of my apartment block, just a 5m

'I'm in favour of reclaiming pavement and that doesn't involve asking nicely.'

x 1m plot to start with,' he says. 'I've grown spinach, red beets, rocket salad, podded peas and all kinds of herbs. Any passersby can take what they desire and my neighbours love it.' Maina plans to expand his range: 'Next spring I'll introduce maize, pumpkin and broad beans. It won't change the world and it's certainly no challenge to capitalist industrial agriculture, but it does bring smiles to faces and plant seeds in people's minds.'

Van der Zwan dug municipal compost into the bed, then built a fence around it to protect it from trampling feet. 'Although it's near a busy street I haven't had a single act of vandalism. The garden is well kept so people think it's official, but I didn't get permission and I'm not planning on asking for it either. I'm in favour of reclaiming the pavement and that doesn't involve asking nicely.'

be a guerrilla gardener

is it legal?

Guerrilla gardening is gardening without permission. You are not technically trespassing as long as you garden on public, not private land. However, gardening on any land without permission can be seen as an act of vandalism. If you are sensible, smile and don't ask for trouble, then local authorities are generally happy to see you take an interest. At the time of writing, no one has ever been arrested for guerilla gardening.

'Some guerrilla gardeners take action at night,' says guerrilla gardener Andrea Bellamy, who regularly seed bombs her neighbourhood in Vancouver, Canada. 'I prefer the "fake it till you make it" approach. In other words, act like you're supposed to be there. If you really want to play the part, bring along a safety vest or other credibility prop.'

be a guerrilla not a terrorist: where to guerrilla garden in the city?

Much as a wish to green your urban environs should be applauded, there are important things to consider before you get happy with the seed bombs. Avoid public parks and gardens since these are generally carefully tended and are best left to the authorities. Any guerrilla gardening you do in such places is likely to be uprooted anyway. Brownfield sites – plots awaiting development, railway sidings and former industrial developments – are also best left as they are. They may look weed-infested and ugly to us, but they're actually doing very well all by themselves with a surprisingly healthy biodiversity of wildflowers and wildlife. Introducing other plants here, say environmentalists, may be no better than well-intentioned vandalism.

Instead, aim for inner-city areas that are already cultivated but in a feeble, half-hearted way. Inner-city

roundabouts, neglected flowerbeds, central reservations, tree pits and forgotten planters – this is where the guerrilla gardener can best make their mark.

In terms of the plants, use common sense. Avoid invasive species such as ivy and mint; it's just bad manners – not to mention environmental hooliganism – to plant something that no one will be able to eradicate. Public areas tend to be far from a tap, so choose plants that don't require much water – lavender is a guerrilla gardening cliché for a reason (see top 10 plants for guerrilla gardening, pages 80–81).

WHAT YOU NEED TO BE A GUERRILLA GARDENER

Thick gardening gloves (have you seen what's in that flowerbed?)

A hand fork or trowel

Seed, plants or seed bombs

A mini watering can (see below)

A carrier bag to remove rubbish from the site

tip When guerrilla gardening, take a plastic litre bottle filled with water, lid on, and a spare lid, perforated with holes. After sowing, screw on the perforated lid to create an instant mini watering can.

roundabouts and central reservations

Roundabouts are often pretty sorry affairs in cities, with bare soil and limping shrubs. This makes them perfect opportunities for the guerrilla gardener, since there is little in the way of weeds to compete with new plantings. The strip running down the centre of busy inner-city roads can be another desolate spot, the odd spindly bush acting as little else than a handy trap for plastic bags. In both cases, think of visual impact. Planting one species en masse can have a much bigger effect than lots of bitty plants. A crowd of tulips or regimental line of sunflowers flanking the road can look stunning.

Roundabouts have an even greater potential for guerrilla gardening. Garden designer Brita von Schoenaich has planted an annual wildflower meadow on the busy Hogarth Roundabout heading westwards on the grim, congested M4 out of London for several years now. Passing motorists are wowed by the waves of poppies, toadflax, cornflowers and scarlet flax that flower from mid summer to mid autumn. It's a splash of bucolic idyll while you sit in a traffic jam.

tree pits, flowerbeds and planters

These diminutive spots are ideal for small-scale guerrilla gardening – lunch-hour incursions if you will. Even if you only have a few minutes, why not pop in a few bulbs, some seed or a couple of plants? You don't need to tell anyone about it, it can be your little secret, to make you smile when you look down from the bus. Planters out of reach of trampling feet and dogs can also be good spots for growing edibles.

top 10 plants for guerrilla gardening

Make a splash and catch the eye of passersby and motorists. All of these will put on a big show.

Bulbs
Easy to plant in the autumn since they need no watering in. Choose from tulips, daffodils, crocuses or snowdrops and plant en masse for the biggest impact.

Meadow annuals
Poppies, cornflowers and marigolds are naturalistic, colourful and easy to sow en masse in spring.

Sunflowers
Who can resist or ignore the happy face of a towering sunflower (below left)? Sow in spring.

Cosmos
Drought-tolerant, this pretty plant will flower for months on end (especially if you deadhead it regularly) and is best in sunny spots. Sow in spring.

Hollyhocks
Tall, cottage-garden style plants that will freely self-seed in sunny spots. Sow in spring.

Lavender
Drought-tolerant and deliciously fragrant. Plant in autumn or spring.

Nasturtiums
Sprawling and drought-tolerant with vivid orange and yellow flowers. Sow in spring.

Erysimum Bowles Mauve
This delightful pink-flowered wallflower (below right) keeps on blooming for months on end. It's perennial and drought-tolerant and will bring in lots of bees. Plant in autumn or spring.

Californian poppies
Stunning orange flowers and silvery foliage, will self-seed. Sow in spring in a sunny site.

Nicotiana sylvestris
Tall plants with elegant white flowers. Particularly fragrant at night. Good in shade.

vegetables and guerilla gardening
Eating vegetables that have grown in close proximity to car exhaust fumes may not seem appealing. But if you can find a spot away from traffic, trampling feet and dogs there is no reason why you can't try a few crops. Take inspiration from Li Tingbang, the 78-year-old Chinese immigrant who tills choy sum and pumpkins in Harlem, New York. Bored of playing mahjong at his old people's home, he found some neglected land behind a bus depot and cultivated it. A wall divides his rows of lettuce and beans from the fumes of rush-hour traffic passing by.

bombs away?

If the thought of navigating three lanes of traffic just to plant some flowers doesn't appeal, don't give up. There is a way to introduce guerrilla gardening in difficult-to-reach areas – such as busy roundabouts or central reservations – without even getting out of the car.

Seed bombing began in the 1970s when the US environmentalist group the Green Guerrillas threw seed bombs – seed put inside condoms, balloons and even glass Christmas baubles – over the fences of abandoned urban lots in New York City. These days, seed bombs are a bit more organic. Seed is generally mixed with compost and potter's clay to form a ball that can carry it into hard-to-reach areas. The clay gradually disintegrates when it rains, allowing the seed to germinate and take root. Try to avoid the temptation of lobbing them over fences into brownfield sites where the seed could disrupt the natural habitat. Seed bombs are best, and the most fun, when thrown into neglected roundabouts, central reservations, flowerbeds and planters when passing by on foot, from a bike or through the car window.

tip Seed bombing is best in spring and autumn when there is generally more rain. Summer seed bombs may be unsuccessful because, unless they get wet, the ball won't disintegrate, preventing any seedlings from growing. Germination will be much improved if you time your seed bombing to occur just before heavy rain so keep an eye on the weather forecast.

10 BEST FLOWERS FOR SEED BOMBS

If combining different kinds of seed in a bomb, make sure they can all be sown at the same time of year. Small seed is best since large seed can make the seed bomb split.

Annual wildflower mixes: meadow annuals such as poppies, marigolds and cornflowers need full sun, while a woodland mix will be happy in a shadier spot.

Californian poppies (*Eschscholzia californica*)

Cosmos

Foxgloves (*Digitalis purpurea*) – beautiful pink, purple or white nodding spires. A woodland plant, good for shady sites.

Hollyhocks (*Alcea*)

Honesty (Lunaria annua) – great for shady sites, purple flowers followed by seed in lovely papery discs.

Nigella – a cottage-garden favourite with blue flowers and beautiful feathery leaves, will self-seed. Best in sun.

Tobacco plant (*Nicotiana sylvestris*)

Verbena bonariensis – tall and airy with purple flowers beloved by bees; a good self-seeder that will soon give a neglected planter a new elegance. Best in sunny spots.

Viper's bugloss (*Echium vulgare*) – towering blue spires that attract bees. Best in sun.

how to MAKE A SEED BOMB

you will need

Flower seed
(see 10 Best Flowers for
Seed Bombs, opposite)

Potter's clay powder – from
any craft shop

Peat-free compost

Water

A bowl

A baking tray

30 minutes

when to do it

Spring or autumn is best,
preferably just before
heavy rain is forecast

how to do it

Mix the seed, clay and compost together in a bowl to a
ratio of three handfuls of clay, five handfuls of compost and
one handful of seed. Then carefully add a little water slowly
and gradually (you don't want it too gloopy), mixing it all
together until you get a consistency that you can form into
conker-sized balls. Lay them out to bake dry on a sunny
windowsill for at least three hours.

tip Before seed bombing,
assess the site to see how
much sun it gets. Choose
your seed accordingly (see
opposite).

BE A STREETSCAPE GARDENER

whose garden is it anyway?

Front gardens are the boundary between the public and private. In the USA, the front lawn is a cultural institution making up 50,000 square miles, the size of the state of Iowa. In Europe, the front garden is traditionally barricaded off with a hedge to stop passersby looking in.

But a new wave of streetscape gardeners is starting to blur that boundary, seeing that little patch between the front door and the street as a chance to amuse or cheer up passersby. Whether it's with 300 tulip bulbs, a row of tomato plants just asking to be picked or a hedge in the shape of a herd of elephants, by planting their front gardens for passersby, they're not only making city streets more colourful, but friendlier and more inclusive too.

RURBANITE: Naomi Schillinger, street gardener, London

Not all street gardeners relish the illicit tag of guerrilla gardening, the seed bombs and the bravado. Some do it in daylight, often with cake. Naomi Schillinger was bored of looking at bare, compacted ground under the trees growing on her street in north London. So she planted them with hollyhocks, wildflowers and lavender. Her neighbours joined in and the trees lining the streets of this busy triangle yards from the screech of the Holloway Road, one of London's screechiest arteries, now emerge from a mass of flowers. Some of the little beds are formal, with bedding plants and chrysanthemums, others cottagey with lofty hollyhocks, and others a joyful tangle of wildflowers. Neighbours have taken ownership of the tree pits, watering and tending them as if they were part of their own garden. Inspired, neighbours started growing vegetables, hollyhocks, even sowing wildflower meadows in their front gardens too. What was once a boring residential street through which people hurried has become a cheerful, friendly place where people stop and chat. Regular cake-and-seed meets on the street are now popular fixtures in the local calendar.

'People want to belong,' says Naomi, in explanation. 'There is a hunger to be part of something in an urban environment, to be on nodding terms with each other so you feel safer and happier.'

Naomi sees tree pits as mini gardens rather than as wild public spaces, and the planting is about entertaining people, giving them an opportunity to stop and look. One of the privet hedges on the street is being shaped into a herd of elephants for the summer. 'Sometimes I'll plant a cauliflower or a cabbage – not to eat, because of the dogs, but just because children love talking about them. They look fantastic.' Up the road, Naomi sowed a wildflower meadow in an empty front garden. Round the corner on busy, grey Holloway Road, she has planted 300 tulip bulbs in a scrubby bit of land outside an office just 'to bring something to the street'. It's 'wow-factor' planting – a little bit of pleasure for anyone who passes by.

'People want to belong'

naomi's tree pit tips

Be careful when digging – try not to damage the roots of any newly planted trees and watch for underground wires.

Edge the pit if you can, and raise the level of soil – John Innes or a mix of garden soil with multipurpose compost works well. But make sure you leave a space around the trunk so the new soil doesn't touch it since this can rot the trunk of even well-established trees.

Young trees are vulnerable so only plant bulbs, small drought-tolerant annuals or shallow-rooted perennials. Around older trees you can plant perennials. Always leave a space of at least 30cm between the plant and the tree trunk.

PROJECT

how to PLANT A TREE PIT FOR SPRING

Planting spring bulbs is perhaps the easiest way to turn a tree pit from boring to beautiful. No soil preparation is necessary apart from digging the holes for the bulbs – you won't even need to weed since the bulbs can be planted among existing vegetation. You can plant a mix of different bulbs, but sticking to one variety makes the biggest impact.

you will need

A garden trowel or bulb planter

About 30 spring-flowering bulbs such as snake's head fritillaries, snowdrops, dog's tooth violet, crocuses, grape hyacinths, winter aconites, native bluebells or tulips

30 minutes

when to do it

Early to late autumn

how to do it

Make a hole for each bulb, taking care to avoid damaging any tree roots. The depth of the planting hole will depend on the bulb – aim for a hole three to four times as deep as the bulb itself. Backfill the holes with soil.

tip Take ownership of newly planted street trees near you by watering them. Many are planted with an irrigation pipe and a large weekly watering of about 5l poured slowly down the pipe will really help them establish.

A TREE PIT WITH IMPACT

This exuberant combination will stop people in their tracks. Despite their eventual size, all these flowers have relatively shallow roots so are ideal for planting in a tree pit. If you can find a tree pit with a fence around the tree, so much the better, since they're perfect for tying the long stems to as they grow.

you will need

A cosmos plant – a tall variety

2 sunflower plants

A hollyhock plant – a single-flowered variety is best

A garden fork

A garden trowel

when to do it

Spring

how to do it

Gently tease out the compacted soil with the garden fork, breaking up any clods of earth and removing stones and rubbish. Dig holes for the plants, leaving at least a foot between them and the tree trunk. Firm in and water well.

TOP FLOWERS TO PLANT IN TREE PITS

SUNNY SPOTS

Alliums

Annual meadow mix wildflowers – such as poppies, cornflowers and marigolds

Cosmos

Hollyhocks (Alcea)

Lavender

Nigella

Oregano

Ox-eye daisy

Rosemary

Sedum spectabile (iceplant)

Sunflowers

Thyme

Verbena bonariensis

SPRING COLOUR

Crocuses – mass plantings look stunning

Daffodils – such as 'Tete a Tete'

Polyanthus

Primroses

Snowdrops

Tulips

SHADY SPOTS

Bluebells

Foxgloves

Honesty (Lunaria annua)

Nicotiana sylvestris

Polypodium ferns

Violas

Woodland wildflower mix

tip Any public planted area in the city is vulnerable to being damaged, whether by vandalism or unintentional trampling by dogs or passers by. Knowing this, limit the chances of horticultural heartbreak by choosing tree pits in quiet residential streets for particularly special planting. If you can ask a neighbour to keep an eye on your efforts by watering and tieing plants in, this will really help their chances too.

how to TURN YOUR FRONT GARDEN INTO AN ANNUAL WILDFLOWER MEADOW

What better gift to your street than turning the patch of scrubby dirt that is your front garden into a wildflower meadow? Bold and beautiful, pictorial meadow seed mixes are all about making a splash. They are a mix of native and non-native annual wildflowers – with no grasses – chosen to make the maximum visual impact. They might include poppies, toadflax, marigolds and larkspur. The beauty of these mixes over native wildflower mixes is that they will flower from mid summer through to late autumn rather than ending their spectacle in mid summer. But you will have to re-sow them every year since they are all annuals. If you want a meadow that will return year after year, see How to Make a Perennial Wildflower Meadow, page 110.

you will need

A patch of lawn – as large as you like (but a 3m square will produce a colourful meadow splash without breaking your back in the preparation) – or bare soil

'Pictorial' wildflower seed mix – look on the internet for a selection

A tape measure

Sensitive kitchen scales

Sand

Bamboo canes (optional)

A garden fork

A garden spade (ideally with a sharp flat blade)

A rake

2 hours to prepare the soil – a gap of 3 weeks – then 15 minutes to sow the meadow

when to do it

Spring

tip If you do not have time to leave the bed for three weeks, you can sow it immediately, but the meadow is likely to be less impressive since weeds such as grasses, thistles, dandelions and ground elder may stop the wildflowers from getting into their stride.

how to do it

If you are turning an area of lawn into meadow, mark it out with a sprinkled line of dry sand or bamboo canes. Remove the turf in manageable sections by pushing your spade down about 3cm and then along just under the grass roots. Short, jabbing motions are more effective than a continuous push. Stack the turfs you remove in an inconspicuous corner, grass-side down, and cover with a piece of carpet or black plastic. Within six months, stacked turfs will break down into a superb fertile topsoil

that you can add to your beds. If you are sowing in bare soil, this preparation stage is unnecessary.

Now dig over the sowing area with your garden fork, removing any stones or roots and breaking up any clods of soil. Rake the soil smooth. You are aiming for a good tilth with no large lumps.

Now walk away and totally ignore it. This allows any dormant weed seed in the soil to germinate. After about three weeks, hoe or pull up the weeds and you are ready to sow.

Measure your sowing area to find out how much seed you'll need (multiplying the length of the two sides to find the number of square metres). If you have an irregular-shaped area, work it out roughly by splitting it up as best you can into 1m squares (you can mark these out with sand). Once you have done this it isn't difficult to work out the approximate area of any bits around the edge, and you can add these in to get to your total.

You sow pictorial seed mixes at a rate of 3g per square metre. So for a 3m square, you'll need 9g. Weigh the seed on your scales and then mix it with an equal amount of sand. The sand shows you where you've already sown, so helping you to spread the seed evenly over the area. Rake in gently. Then tread over the area and water well.

what next?

You shouldn't have to water your meadow again unless there is a prolonged dry spell. By the end of the season (which is late autumn) cut down and remove the dead stems. If you want to re-sow the following year, repeat the soil preparation in spring.

other ideas for reclaiming your street

Call your local authority and ask them to plant trees on your street – especially edible fruit trees such as cherries, apples, pears or crab apples that people living on the street can harvest together. Snip your hedge into an eye-catching shape – elephant, train, Loch Ness monster – whatever will make people smile. Train eye-catching edible crops such as tomatoes, pumpkins or runner beans along the fence so they are within easy reach of passersby. They will make people stop and talk and, if they take some, who cares? Maybe it'll give them an idea for next year.

be a wildlife gardener

You might assume your balcony or patio garden is devoid of wildlife, but cities are surprisingly comfy habitats for animals. Who hasn't marvelled at the sinuous progress of a fox making its way across an urban street at dusk? Or the chutzpah of a city squirrel raiding a garden bird feeder? We may think we live in a concrete jungle, but it's one in which a lot of wildlife, from birds to insects, feel at home.

We think of farmland as being 'good' for nature and cities as being 'bad', but this isn't the real picture. The UK has lost 97 per cent of its flowering meadows since the Second World War – habitats where bees and other pollinating insects thrived. Even between 1970 and 2000 the diversity of species of flora and fauna in European farmland declined by 23 per cent. Meanwhile in the US, 30 per cent of native flora is considered to be at risk of vanishing forever. If you look to cities, however, brownfield sites – areas of disused industrial or commercial land – have become a haven for endangered species, from toads and snakes to song thrushes, hedgehogs and rare bees. The irony is that you are more likely to see a rich diversity of insects and wildflowers in a scrappy-looking bit of land under a railway arch than you might on farmland blitzed with insecticides and weedkillers.

But we shouldn't take urban biodiversity for granted. The world's cities are growing larger and more populous every day. The green and brownfield gaps in the buildings and roads are being ever more squeezed by new housing developments. City gardens are getting smaller as people pave over their front gardens for parking and extend their houses at the back. Every year London loses to development an area of gardens equal to two and a half times the size of Hyde Park. Now, more than ever, we need to make sure we are leaving some space for the wildlife that lives in our cities, not just because it needs us, but because we – in our deskbound, technocentric lives – need it.

The more man-made our environment, the more precious it seems when we find it – a butterfly landing on sedum, a spider spinning a web high up on traffic lights. Humankind has been on this earth for hundreds of thousands of years yet has only been urban for a few centuries. It's not surprising we still yearn for a closeness to wild things.

Start treating your outside space, garden, balcony or windowsills, as a miniature nature reserve and you will get close to more insects and birds than you thought possible. Here are some ideas to bring urban wildlife in...

if you do just three things to attract urban wildlife…

let some of your lawn grow long (see page 104)

make a pond (see page 96)

plant nectar-rich flowers (see page 101)

RURBANITE: Keith Reynolds, balcony wildlife gardener, Manchester

A wildlife garden doesn't have to be big, and at just 1.4m x 2m, Keith Reynolds' balcony in Hulme, Manchester, proves it. Ladybirds, bees, parasitic wasps, caterpillars and butterflies all now hang out at Keith's mini wildlife reserve. They take advantage of the native flowers he has crammed into galvanised buckets – garlic mustard, cornfield annuals, mint and cuckooflower – and spring bulbs such as crocuses and bluebells. A birdbath made from an old saucepan is propped on the railings, while an upturned dustbin lid makes a handy mini wildflower meadow, filled with the bee-magnet, bird's foot trefoil. A climbing evergreen honeysuckle provides nectar for bees as well as cover and berries for birds.

> 'It turns a dead, sterile space into something that's alive and interesting.'

Keith's balcony is an anomaly in this area. The other balconies in his block of flats are bare, the gardens gravel deserts. When he first moved here, his bird feeders went unvisited. Keith pushed the council to plant crab apple trees nearby and thanks to these and the greenery on his balcony, coal tits, great tits, robins and pigeons now regularly stop by. Since the second-floor balcony is pretty windy, Keith put willow screening around the railings as a windbreak. The leftover screening made a great bee hotel, rolled up and placed in a sunny spot. Last year he was delighted to see some of the ends of the hollow stems had been sealed up by mud, evidence that solitary bees had laid eggs inside. A wooden garden ornament in the shape of a mushroom has been transformed into another potential insect nest for hoverflies, bees or solitary wasps by drilling holes of various sizes into the wood.

This is wildlife gardening up close. Keith, who moved here from a large garden three years ago, knows every centimetre of his space and notices every arrival. 'In a big garden it's easy to miss the fine details because you're not looking closely. But, here, I'll pick up a leaf and see a moth has rolled up in it. I've watched a potter wasp carrying off a caterpillar.' He regularly spots mice scaling the vertical brick wall outside to reach the nasturtium seedpods in his windowboxes and marvels at the colony of large white butterflies on the leaves.

'For me, it's about the biodiversity, about welcoming nature to my doorstep as opposed to shooing it away. I love sitting out having my breakfast on the balcony while the bees and butterflies have their breakfast too.'

Be nice to nettles

A pot of stinging nettles might seem a curious thing to grow on a balcony or terrace, but if you want to attract wildlife they're a surefire winner, since they attract 40 species of insect. The aphids that will live on them all year round are host-specific so won't bother other plants, but will provide food for ladybirds. The leaves themselves are a food source for the caterpillars of red admiral, peacock, small tortoiseshell and comma butterflies. Your plants will benefit from a feed made by steeping nettle leaves in water for a couple of weeks. And you can eat nettles too – as a side vegetable or in a delicious soup (see page 129).

Running in the corridor

You may be all too aware of the boundaries of your little garden, balcony or roof terrace, marking out your territory in the big city, but urban wildlife won't see it that way. To the frogs, hedgehogs, mice, birds, bees and other insects living around you, your garden is just a small stepping stone through which they will pass on their way to somewhere else, stopping off for a drink, something to eat or a rest. Windowboxes can be perfect rest stops for bees and butterflies. Start to see your outside space as part of a wider wildlife corridor connecting brownfield sites, parks and other gardens, and you will understand the natural world of your city much better.

The hole truth

Solid fencing is a 'Berlin Wall' to wandering animals – an impenetrable barrier through which they cannot pass. If you have such fencing in your garden, dig a few holes under it if you can (about 12cm square). If you're putting up new fencing, consider picket-style fencing instead.

how to MAKE A WILDFLOWER MEADOW IN A DUSTBIN LID

If you garden in a small space such as a city balcony, this is a great way to grow a relatively wide range of sun-loving wildflowers such as poppies, marigolds, cornflowers, corncockle, chamomile and bird's foot trefoil. Prop the lid in a pot and it will be quite stable. For tiny spaces, it can protrude over the railings to give you extra growing space. Look out for old dustbin lids on skips.

you will need

A dustbin lid (either plastic or metal), the deeper the better

A drill

Water-retaining granules (optional)

Peat-free multipurpose compost

Wildflower seed – ideally a mixture of annuals for colour in the first year and perennials that will establish over time

when to do it

Either from late summer to mid autumn or in spring

how to do it

Drill several holes in the lid, at least 0.5cm in diameter. Then add compost with a handful of water-retaining granules. These are beneficial in a container as shallow as this since they stop the compost drying out too quickly. Sprinkle the seed on the surface of the compost, and press them in with the heel of your hand so they are in good contact with the compost. Water well and place in a sunny, sheltered spot.

MAKE A WILDLIFE POND IN A POT

If you want to do one thing in your inner-city garden to bring in wildlife, make a pond. They're a magnet and a haven for wildlife, from dragonflies and waterboatmen to spawning frogs, bees having a drink and birds wanting a quick dip. All you need is a watertight, frost-proof container and some pond plants, and the wildlife will eventually stop by. Even if you live several storeys up there's no reason why you can't make a pond, though you'd be lucky to find any frogs that can climb that high.

you will need

A watertight, frost-proof container, wider than it is tall, around 60cm x 80cm; galvanised baths are ideal – look in junk shops or vintage stores

Around seven pond plants – a mix of oxygenating plants that lie under water, surface plants that float on top and emergent plants that grow above the surface. For example:

A handful of hornwort

A handful of starwort

A water forget-me-not

A marsh marigold

A European brooklime

An arrowhead

A cottongrass plant

Bricks, stones or terracotta pots to raise the plants to the correct levels and provide access for wildlife

Half an hour

when to do it

Early spring to mid autumn

how to do it

Fill your container with water – ideally rainwater. Place the oxygenating and surface plants (in this case hornwort and starwort) straight into the water. Then place your potted pond plants into the pond. They should come in mesh baskets ready to pop into the water – if not, plant in aquatic compost in pond baskets, available from garden centres. Stand the pots on bricks or upturned pots so the top of the compost is at the required depth for the variety. Now make sure frogs and toads can get into your pond by placing stones, bricks or plant pots both outside and inside the pond to provide an easy climbing surface. It's also a good idea to provide a perch within the pond for birds and bees to land on when they come for a drink. A large stone that juts out of the water is ideal.

tip It doesn't matter if the surface of the pond freezes over winter, but it's not a good idea if the whole thing freezes solid. In harsh winters put a ping-pong ball in the pond – its constant motion will stop the water freezing solid.

tip If you include oxygenating plants in your pond, the water should remain clear, but if algae do grow, add barley straw extract (available from all garden centres) or throw in a handful of watercress from the supermarket. It will soon grow roots and is an oxygenating plant so will keep the water clear. Thin the watercress out from time to time to prevent it taking over.

3 more things to attract urban wildlife...

Don't use insecticides – they kill butterflies and many pollinating insects, as well as ladybirds, ground beetles and spiders. When aphids congregate on a plant, it's never long before the ladybird cavalry arrive to munch them. Use organic slug pellets only if you absolutely have to (around vulnerable young vegetables, for example).

Provide food for birds by growing bushes and flowers whose berries or seedheads they can eat (see pages 114–115).

Don't tidy up your garden until mid spring – seedheads are eaten by birds while all that brown dead foliage is great shelter for insects, mice, frogs, hedgehogs and toads.

Plant it and they will come. Bringing bees into your garden, balcony or roof garden is easy, however urban your surroundings. It is also hugely improtant since a healthy worldwide population of bees means wild flowers and crops are pollinated – vital for the survival of mankind. Cities are excellent habitats for bees, providing a great variety of flowering plants blooming from early spring right through to the end of autumn.

Recent research has firmly linked a group of agricultural insecticides called neonicotinoids with a decline in the world bee population. Widely used in Europe and the USA (99.8 per cent of maize seed sown in the USA is treated with neonicotinoids), these chemicals, which are a type of nerve poison, are highly effective in killing insects that are pests to crops. Unfortunately, there is also now clear evidence

that they are harmful to bees, affecting their ability to navigate and form new queens. Cities are refuges from this agricultural chemical warfare. Keeping a beehive in the city is therefore not only a fascinating hobby, but also a really important step towards helping honeybees worldwide (see Keep... Bees, page 158).

But you don't have to invest in a beekeeper suit to help bees. Much pollination is done by solitary wild bees, which don't live in hives but nest in hollow stems. Bumblebees, which nest in old mouse holes and other dry burrows, do a valuable service too, and really need our help. In North America, several once-common bumblebee species have disappeared, while in Britain three species have become extinct in the past 80 years. Here's how to encourage both solitary bees and bumblebees into your garden, however small...

MAKE A SOLITARY BEE HOTEL

Small and often black, solitary bees might not look like your classic bee, but they are the unsung heroes of the bee world. In fact, about 90 per cent of bees worldwide are solitary bees. While honeybees get all the glory and bumblebees have cornered the cuteness vote, these unassuming, non-aggressive little creatures are busy pollinating flowers – and particularly fruit blossom – at a prodigious rate. One red mason bee can do the job of 12 honeybees. Don't think you have to identify them all; there are 250 species in Britain and Europe, and even more in the USA.

While honeybees live in hives and bumblebees nest in the ground, solitary bees lay single eggs in nest cells in dead wood and hollow stems. It's easy to replicate this environment with a wooden box, some hollow stems such as bamboo, bramble, teasels, elder and raspberry and blocks of wood with drilled holes. It might also attract leafcutter bees, lacewings, hoverflies and ladybirds looking for nests or shelter.

A bee hotel doesn't have to be in a box – any crevice or hole in the wall can be exploited by adding a few hollow stems. You can even tuck bundles of stems between windowboxes.

you will need

1 wooden wine crate; if you can't find a wine crate, look around for old drawers or make your own box out of planks of wood

2 or 3 blocks of wood – make sure the wood hasn't been treated with preservative

Plenty of hollow stems such as brambles, raspberries, elder, teasel, cosmos, rose or bamboo; rolled-up reed or bamboo screening works well too

A saw

Secateurs

Garden twine

Sandpaper

A drill with varying drill bits from 2mm to 10mm diameter

A piece of plastic pond liner or strong plastic rubble bag cut slightly larger than the 'roof' side of the box

Drawing pins or a stapler

Strong eyelets, nails, screws and strong wire (if hanging from a wall)

About 3 hours

when to do it

Do this any time of year, although bees will start looking for somewhere to lay their eggs at the end of summer.

how to do it

Cut the stems and blocks of wood so that they are just a little shorter than the depth of the box. When cutting the bamboo cut below a node so there is a decent hollow length. Roll up any reed or bamboo screening and cut to the right length. Start placing the stems in the box interspersed with logs until the box is packed tightly. Then drill plenty of holes in the wooden blocks varying the holes from 2mm to 10mm. Secure the pond liner to the 'roof' of the box with drawing pins or staples. Then trim the liner to size leaving a short overhang at the front.

where to put it

Bees need warmth so place the hotel in a position facing south or south-east. Standing it on a garden wall, shed or shelf is the easiest option since the box is heavy. Raise it up on bricks or pieces of wood to avoid rain splashing up inside into the box and tilt it forwards slightly so that rain falls off the roof front.

If you are hanging the box from a wall or fence, fix it at least a metre above the ground making sure there is no foliage in front of it (this puts the bees off making it their home). Attach the eyelets towards to the top end of the box, then thread strong wire through them and hang the wire up to a strong hook or nail on the wall.

what next?

From early summer mason bees – such as the red mason bee with its red rear – may be the first guests to drop by. They'll make a series of cells in the holes and leave pollen and an egg in each cell before blocking up the entrance with mud. Later in the summer leafcutter bees may check in. They will line and then block up their stems or holes with circles of leaves they have cut from wild rose bushes. In midsummer, the smallest holes might attract harebell bees. Look out also for ladybirds and lacewings.

You can leave your bee hotel in situ over winter as long as it doesn't get wet. The roof liner will protect the top of the box from the weather, but if rain is getting into the front, it would be preferable to move it somewhere cold and dry throughout autumn and winter – a garden shed would be ideal.

how to MAKE A NESTING SITE FOR BUMBLEBEES

In spring it's not unusual to see a bumblebee queen inside the house acting oddly, flying slowly and disappearing into corners or even pockets. She's looking for a nest site – and will usually go on to find one in an old mouse hole or the base of an untidy hedge. If she doesn't have any pollen on her back legs it's a sign that she hasn't yet found a suitable site. Why not make her one?

you will need

A garden

A paving slab (around 50 x 50 cm is ideal)

A trowel or spade

Chicken wire (about 30cm square)

Hamster bedding (if you have a pet hamster, use old bedding, since the smell can attract

bumblebees – if not, just buy it from a pet shop)

Bamboo cane, about 2 cm in diameter

30 minutes

when to do it

All year, though bumblebees will be looking for nesting sites from late winter to mid spring

how to do it

Choose a relatively undisturbed site in the garden out of direct sunlight, ideally along a hedge, fence or wall. Dig a hole about 15 cm deep and 30 cm wide. Scrunch up the chicken wire into a bird's-nest shape and put it at the bottom of the hole (this helps with ventilation and prevents the bedding from becoming waterlogged). Next lay a few handfuls of hamster bedding on top of the wire nest. Place the paving slab over the hole. Now poke the cane down the side of the slab and into the hole to make an entrance tunnel (about 2 cm wide) for the bees. Remove the cane. Then cross your fingers that a bumblebee queen will want to make it home.

tip Block it out. To attract bees and butterflies, plant the same flowers together in blocks rather than dotting them all over the garden. Bees and other pollinating insects are more likely to notice them.

tip Flowers in sunny positions are much more attractive to bees.

which flowers do bees like best?

Avoid double-flowered plants: those overbred specimens with frou-frou petals might be beautiful to the 'perfectly-kept-gardens' brigade, but the bees can't find their way through all the petals to get to the nectar and pollen. Avoid most annual bedding plants such as pelargoniums, busy Lizzies and begonias, which have no nectar and pollen in them, so are useless to bees. Instead choose traditional cottage flowers with simple blooms or native wildflowers.

Bees need nectar for much of the year. Urban gardeners are increasingly seeing bees venturing out on mild days in winter so try to include something that flowers in the coldest months.

8

SPRING FLOWERS FOR BEES

Crocuses
Forget-me-not
Fruit tree blossom
Grape hyacinth
Hellebores
Rosemary
Strawberries
Violets

PLANT A SPRING WINDOWBOX FIT FOR A QUEEN

Spring is an important time, particularly for bumblebee queens emerging from hibernation. Only the queen survives the winter so, by providing nectar you are not only helping her, but also ensuring a whole new colony thrives. Unlike honeybees, bumblebees do not have a large store of honey in their nest so are vulnerable early in the season. If they don't find nectar they cannot fly and will die. This rather handsome spring windowbox is a great early source of nectar and pollen.

you will need

A large windowbox at least 60cm long and 20cm deep

Some soil-based compost such as John Innes no. 2

2 hellebore plants such as *Helleborus niger*

About 20 Muscari (grape hyacinth) bulbs

2 pots of primroses (*Primula vulgaris*), oxlips (*Primula oliator*) or cowslips (*Primula veris*)

when to do it

Autumn

how to do it

Fill the windowbox with compost, then plant the hellebores in the centre and the primroses, oxlips or cowslips on either end. Plant the remaining spaces with the muscari bulbs (about 5cm apart at a depth of about double the bulb length). Water well and place in a sunny, sheltered spot. All of these plants will come back year after year if you don't let the container dry out.

8

EARLY SUMMER FLOWERS FOR BEES

Alliums
Broad beans
Campanula
Foxgloves
Raspberries
Stachys
Thyme
Viper's bugloss

MID SUMMER FLOWERS FOR BEES

Astrantia
Blackberries
Borage
Fennel
Lavender
Oregano
Runner beans
Sunflowers

LATE SUMMER & AUTUMN FLOWERS FOR BEES

Aster
Dahlia (single-flowered)
Echinacea
Eryngium gigantium (Miss
  Wilmott's ghost)
Rudbeckia
Scabious
Sedum spectabile (iceplant)
Verbena bonariensis

WINTER FLOWERS FOR BEES

Cyclamen
Daphnes
Hellebores
Primroses
Snowdrops
Violas
Winter aconite
Winter-flowering
  honeysuckle

MAKE A ONE-STOP SHOP FOR BEES

This project not only looks fantastic on a balcony, patio or roof terrace, but in just one container it provides nectar and pollen for bees all year round. If you can't find a galvanised bathtub, try using a rubber tubtrug (widely available in supermarkets), a trough or a half barrel.

you will need

1 large container such as an old galvanised bath, tubtrug or half barrel, about 80cm x 60cm and at least 30cm deep

A hellebore

A trailing rosemary (*Rosmarinus prostratus*)

15 crocus bulbs

A lavender plant

A trailing thyme

A trailing oregano

A *Verbena bonariensis*

A *Sedum spectabile* (ice plant)

Multipurpose compost

40 minutes

when to do it

Autumn

how to do it

Make sure the container already has drainage holes and, if not, drill about eight holes in the bottom. Then fill with compost to about 10cm from the top. Plant the rosemary, oregano and thyme at the edges of the container so they can trail down outside. Then plant the verbena towards the back and the other plants and bulbs throughout the rest of the space. Top up with more compost so it is almost to the top and water well. Place in a sunny, sheltered spot.

make your lawn bee-friendly

Try leaving an area of your lawn unmown between late June and early August. It will burst into life with bird's foot trefoil and red clover, both magnets to bees. When you do mow this area, remove any clippings from the grass. This keeps the fertility of the soil low, which wildflowers tend to prefer. Leaving an area of your lawn long will encourage other animals too – hedgehogs like to forage in long grass and butterflies will lay their eggs there.

GROW TO... GREEN YOUR ROOF

A bird's eye view of any developed city would reveal a patchwork of grey and black – vast areas of concrete, roof felt, lead, tile and glass – on to which the sun relentlessly burns and from which rainwater pours straight into overworked city drains. Large city buildings act like storage heaters, retaining the heat of the sun during the day and then releasing it at night. The result is the 'urban heat island' effect in which the temperature of cities is several degrees warmer than the surrounding countryside, leading to an increased dependence on energy-guzzling air-conditioning.

City roofs can also cause local flash flooding, as sudden downpours rush straight off them and overwhelm the drains. In the case of cities that installed their drainage systems before the 1930s – New York City, Washington DC, Seattle and London – this can only be dealt with by releasing untreated water mixed with sewage straight into local rivers. This, in turn, kills fish and pollutes the water. Just 20 minutes of heavy rain is enough to start water from toilets flowing into Brooklyn's waterways. Around 60 times a year, raw sewage is discharged into London's River Thames, making the water a health hazard and killing fish, as the Victorian sewers struggle to cope with heavy rainfall. In 2004, a particularly heavy downpour caused 600,000 tonnes of untreated sewage to be dumped into the Thames, leaving around 100,000 fish dead.

But imagine if the bird's eye patchwork was green. If green roofs were adopted in cities on a large scale they would cool buildings, reducing air-conditioning costs by at least 10 per cent. A recent study in the USA found that green roofs in Queens, New York, planted with sedum cut the rate of heat gained through the roof in summer by 84 per cent. Green roofs also store rainwater. At least half of the rainwater falling on a green roof never makes it to ground level since it is used by the plants growing there or gradually evaporates back into the atmosphere. Any water that does reach the ground has been sufficiently delayed that it won't contribute to flash flooding. The UK's Environment Agency sees green roofs as a major way to combat storm run-off – a problem likely to grow thanks to climate change – and is pushing to convert more of London's 2,500 hectares of existing flat roof space into green roofs.

But these aren't the only reasons to embrace the greening of roofs in our cities: green roofs also increase biodiversity, allowing local wildlife and flora to thrive. In a recent Swiss study, a green roof in Basel was found to support 79 beetle and 40 spider species, 20 of which were rare. If you think that the footprint of every city building was once land into which rain soaked and on which vegetation grew, putting a green roof on it is just recreating the habitat that was lost, but transplanting it several storeys up. The roof of a large office block could, in fact, be an even more desirable place for wildlife than ground level – after all, who is going to clean away a spider's web or disturb a nesting redstart 25 storeys up?

how to PUT A GREEN ROOF ON YOUR GARDEN SHED

Let's be honest, greening your little garden shed is unlikely to make much of an impact on the urban heat island effect. But it will increase biodiversity, attract insects and reduce rainwater run-off. And, of course, perhaps most importantly, it will look beautiful. Whether it's a shed, a bicycle shelter, a chicken coop, a bin store or a bird house, many of us have wooden structures in our gardens that are just crying out for a green roof makeover. Rather than looking at boring grey roof felt, you could be gazing at a waving throng of ox-eye daisies or blood-red poppies. Here's how to do it.

you will need

Pond liner a little larger than your roof area

Water-retentive matting such as capillary matting

Fencing featherboards 15 cm wide for a wildflower roof, 10 cm wide for a sedum roof (see What Kind of Green Roof? page 108)

Timber battens to reinforce the frame

A saw

A tape measure

Scissors

A drill

Galvanised tacks

Galvanised screws

Galvanised metal brackets and screws to hold the frame to the wall (if a sloping roof)

3 hours if you're new to DIY, 1 hour for a pro

when to do it

Any time

how to do it

Place the pond liner over the roof so that it hangs over the sides and tack it to the edges, cutting off any excess with scissors. Place the capillary matting on top and cut to fit. Next, measure each plane of your roof and construct a frame from your featherboards and timber battens to these exact dimensions. Reinforce the frame internally to create a grid pattern so there are several pockets to plant in. Place the frame on top of the shed roof.

Water needs to be able to drain off the roof freely. You can ensure this either by propping the lower edge of the frame up on 1cm timber wedges or cutting triangular holes in the frame with the saw. If the shed is against a wall or fence, you may want to secure it to the wall with L-shaped brackets to stop it slipping off. Alternatively, fix the frame to the roof by nailing through the internal battens.

is your shed strong enough?

Any structure can have a green roof as long as it is strong enough to hold it up. Is yours? Typical green roofs weigh between 60 and 150 kg per square metre so bear this in mind when considering your structure. For small projects such as bird tables, you won't need to do any preparation, but garden sheds will probably need strengthening. Lengths of timber should be cut and wedged vertically into the internal frame of the shed to reinforce it. It may also be necessary to strengthen the roof with a piece of plywood, screwing it down with galvanised screws.

how to plant a green roof

If possible, get hold of a specialist green roof substrate – try the internet for local suppliers. These are mostly inorganic matter – crushed brick or expanded clay – so are light and low in nutrients. If you can't find any, you can improvise by mixing a soil-based compost, such as John Innes no. 2, in a 50:50 ratio with Perlite.

Before adding the substrate, lay 'crocks', such as pieces of broken-up polystyrene or pebbles, next to the drainage holes to stop compost clogging them up. If you wrap these crocks in horticultural fleece they won't fall through the holes. Now you can fill the frame with your substrate and you are ready to plant.

what kind of green roof?

A carpet of sedum or an exuberant tangle of wildflowers? Or maybe you'd prefer a crop of strawberries from on high? How you choose to plant your green roof is up to you. Here are some options...

sedum is the green roof equivalent of a lawn – neat, uniform and extremely popular.
Pros: Easy to install – usually arriving as a pre-grown blanket that you roll out. Needs only 5–7cm of substrate so a deep frame is unnecessary. Expect succulent, 'bubbly' leaves all year round from green to red, and flowers that are yellow, white and pink that bees love. Extraordinary drought tolerance so you probably won't need to water it once it's established.
Cons: Sedum has fewer visual fireworks than a wildflower roof.

An *edible* roof should thrive as long as it's at least 15cm deep and planted with crops that are shallow-rooting. These would include spreading, drought-tolerant herbs such as thyme and oregano which look lovely trailing over the edge of the roof, especially when mixed with wild strawberries. Chives, basil, coriander, salad rocket and even lettuces should thrive if you water regularly.

Pros: Novel, fun and a productive use of space in a small garden.
Cons: You will have to water even when established, and harvesters will need a head for heights...

A '*brownfield*' roof mimics the wildlife-rich habitat of urban wasteland on a small scale. Before planting, create mini troughs and mounds in the roof substrate to make a more varied terrain and act as shelter for insects, birds and invertebrates. Include pools for rainwater to collect into, whether simply by forming a piece of pond liner into a saucer shape or including a lid or bowl. Add pieces of wood, brick, stone or rope to encourage nesting animals. In time, wildflowers will seed, either blown in by the wind or dropped by birds.
Pros: Great for biodiversity; it's fascinating to see what plants turn up as nature takes its course. Low maintenance.
Cons: Brown, not green (at least until plants establish themselves). Bit scruffy for some.

A *wildflower* roof roots your building firmly in its local environment, whether it's a bike store crowned with marigolds, corn poppies and ox-eye daisies or a garden shed topped by viper's bugloss and greater knapweed.
Pros: A great way to bring native wildflowers into your garden. Annual cornfield mixes look particularly splashy, with dramatic red annual poppies, corn marigolds and ox-eye daisies. Mix with perennial wildflowers for long-term success. Good for pollinating insects and biodiversity in general.
Cons: It is inconsistent: after flowering (from mid to late summer) much of the roof will look brown until the following spring.

go wild on the roof

Want to make a splash with your wildflower roof? Here are some design ideas for both sunny and shady sites.

Spring greens

On sunny roofs, bring in the bees early in the season with cowslips, dwarf narcissus, crocuses and muscari, bejewelling a roof with bright blue clusters. In shadier positions, delicate deep purple dog violets, enchanter's nightshade, bluebells, oxlips and primroses will thrive, bringing a hint of the woodland floor, while red campion will loll gracefully over everything else with its profusion of delicate pink flowers.

Lofty drama queens

For impact on sunny sites, go for blood-red field poppies, raggedy orange corn marigolds, meadow clary and viper's bugloss, both of which have stunning spires of blue flowers that bees adore. The lofty pale yellow flowers of evening primrose are a magnet to moths. In late summer greater mullein will dominate any roof with its towering spire of yellow flowers and felty leaves. In shadier sites, the columbine will steal the show, its graceful stems topped with exquisite purple clusters, clearing the stage for the later-flowering Welsh poppy and its handsome bright yellow petals.

Airy fairy

To hold a wildflower roof together you need some wiry-stemmed plants to weave in among the others and give the roof a glorious look of tangly profusion. Ox-eye daisies, yarrow, tough hawkbit, red valerian, blue fleabane and greater knapweed all do the job wonderfully. Shadier roofs are great places for the greater stitchwort with its spidery stems and profusion of white stars that flower for months on end.

Low and trailing

Any green roof needs a low-growing layer and some trailing plants to soften the edges. For sunny roofs, choose from biting stonecrop, wild thyme, white clover, wild chamomile, wild strawberry, bird's foot trefoil or sweet alyssum. Shady roofs are good places for the pink flowers of herb Robert and the barren strawberry, which is fruitless, but has pretty white flowers.

collect wildflower seed for your roof

If you have lots of wildflowers growing near you, why not collect a few seed to sprinkle on your roof? If you take only a few seed from common species, you won't be doing any harm (see How to Collect and Save Seed, page 63).

how to put a
GREEN ROOF ON YOUR BIRD TABLE

If greening your shed roof seems a little daunting, why not give your bird table a green makeover instead? It'll make it more interesting, and when the sedum is in bloom, the bees will come flocking too.

you will need

A timber batten	Galvanised screws
Pond liner or a rubble bag	A hammer
Water-retentive or capillary matting, enough for a double layer over the roof	Sedum matting (1 square metre will be more than enough)
A saw	Scissors
A drill	A couple of hours
Galvanised tacks	

when to do it

Any time of year

how to do it

Measure the roof and cut the plastic liner to fit it, then place it over the roof and secure with tacks. Cut the matting to fit the roof and then repeat so you have two identical pieces. Lay both pieces on top of the liner so you have a double layer (this helps keep the roots moist). Then divide the timber batten into four pieces, one for each slope of the roof. Cut one end of each piece to 45 degrees so they fit neatly at the apex of the roof. Drill some pilot holes into the timber and then screw them into the roof. Next cut the sedum matting to size and lay it on top of the roof. After an initial watering it shouldn't be necessary to water it again unless you have a prolonged dry spell. Place it in a sunny spot.

Sedum is best for such a small structure because it is so drought-tolerant and only needs a thin layer of compost to grow in. You can buy the sedum matting online.

how to MAKE A PERENNIAL WILDFLOWER MEADOW

Few rural sights can deliver the wow factor of a native wildflower meadow in full bloom. The only trouble is, you'd be hard pushed to find one these days since modern agricultural methods have made these flower-rich habitats increasingly scarce. All the more reason to try to recreate such a sight in the city, and even on a balcony (see page 94). If it's purely visual fireworks you're after, a pictorial or non-native annual flower mix is for you (see page 88). But, if you want a long-term more sustainable meadow you need a native mixture of grasses, annual flowers and perennials. This provides habitats and food as well as nectar for bees and butterflies. It takes some time for the perennial flowers to establish, but if you add some cornfield annuals for colour into the sowing mix it will look beautiful from the first year.

you will need

Native perennial wildflower meadow seed (look online for native seed mixes, making sure they are locally grown)

Native cornfield annual seed

A patch of lawn

A garden spade

A garden fork

A couple of hours

when to do it

From late summer to mid-autumn or in spring

how to do it

Prepare the soil as for the How to Turn Your Front Lawn into an Annual Wildflower Meadow project (see page 88). Now take half the seed and broadcast it over the area in one direction at a rate of about 4g per square metre. Then broadcast the other half of the seed at right angles to the first lot to ensure an even spread. Do not cover the seed with soil. Tread over the area and water well.

what next?

In the first year, cut the meadow to a height of 5cm every time it reaches 10–20cm. This stops any annual weeds from flowering, meaning they won't return next year. From then on, only mow once a year in late summer, with a subsequent cut in the autumn. Make sure you remove the grass clippings to keep the soil fertility down.

tip The lazy wildflower meadow aka the overgrown plot. Of course, you don't actually have to sow anything to create a wildflower garden of sorts. Nature will do it for you. The easiest way to bring native wild flowers and wildlife into your garden is simply to leave an area to go wild. But keep thistles, nettles and brambles in check since these will swamp other species.

GROW TO... BRING IN URBAN BIRDS

Birds want food, shelter and water, and it's easy to provide all three in even a tiny urban garden. If you want to attract birds, put up bird feeders and plant flowers whose berries or seedheads they're fond of and in whose branches they can shelter or nest. If you have space, consider planting a tree or hedge. A wildlife pond will also have the local bird life dropping in for a quick dip and a drink (see Make a Wildlife Pond in a Pot, page 96).

5 TOP PLANTS FOR URBAN BIRDS

Cotoneaster bushes are stripped bare of their berries every winter – blackbirds particularly love them.

Honeysuckle berries are swooped on by thrushes and finches; thrushes nest in the thicket of climbing stems and aphids provide food too.

Blackberry or bramble bushes are a win–win for the urbanite wildlife lover since both you and the birds can eat the berries, and there are a lot to go round. Choose a thornless variety such as Oregon Thornless to save your fingers.

Ivy berries are snapped up by birds in the winter when there is little else to eat. The twining stems also provide great shelter and nesting opportunities for wrens and blackbirds.

Dog rose shoots are covered with aphids in spring, a tasty snack for great tits, blue tits and other insect eaters. The thicket of thorny stems is good cover for birds too.

GO TO SEED IN A POT

Seedheads are popular snacks for finches and sparrows so try to remember to leave them on your garden plants over winter – they look good too, catching the low winter sun or encased in frost. This pot looks great in summer, the sunflowers towering over pink honesty flowers that turn into papery discs. The spiky blue globe thistle or *Echinops ritro* attracts hordes of insects and provides an architectural kick. The sunflowers and honesty will self-seed readily, while the echinops is a perennial so will last several years – divide congested clumps in the spring.

you will need

A large pot at least 45cm in diameter and 30cm deep (a half barrel is ideal)

5 sunflower plants – a medium-height variety is best to avoid extremely long supports

A globe thistle (*Echinop ritro*) plant

5 honesty (*Lunaria annua*) plants

Multipurpose peat-free compost

when to do it

Spring

how to do it

Fill the pot to within 10cm of the top then plant the sunflowers in the pattern of a five on a die. Fill in the gaps with the other plants. Water well.

GROW TO... BRING IN THE BUTTERFLIES

Butterfly names sound as light and airy as they are – think of holly blue, clouded yellow, orange tip. These are the urban gardener's favourite skittish guests, dropping by unannounced and often leaving just as abruptly, flitting over the fence or balcony railings in a freewheeling dance. Butterflies are considered a wildlife marker species, since they are susceptible to tiny changes in air quality and climate. They are the 'yellow canary' of the wildlife world – telling us when things are changing before we can sense it ourselves. Their favoured habitats – mainly meadows, prairies and grasslands – have been destroyed on a massive scale, and are now all but absent, for example, in the lower 48 states of the USA. Global warming may also be damaging their numbers, with rising temperatures putting butterflies out of sync with their food plants. In the UK, 72 per cent of UK butterfly species are in decline. Almost one in ten European butterfly species is currently at risk of extinction. In the USA, 23 species are on the danger list.

But urban habitats can be refuges for butterflies, with nectar-rich gardens and brownfield sites particularly appealing. The buddleia bush, that mainstay of the abandoned urban plot, is known as the butterfly bush for good reason. We need to look after the butterflies in our urban gardens, terraces and balconies. Planting things they like to eat is a great first step...

choose nectar-rich plants
Buddleia is far and away the favoured plant for butterflies, popular with 18 species, from brimstones and gatekeepers to red admirals and small coppers. If you live in a built-up urban area, however, chances are there will be plenty of buddleia growing in brownfield and neglected sites around you. So why not choose from this list, right, instead?

10
BEST NECTAR PLANTS FOR BUTTERFLIES

Erysimum Bowles's Mauve
Iceplant (*Sedum spectabile*)
Field scabious
Honesty (*Lunaria annua*)
Lavender
Mint
Oregano
Red valerian
Sweet rocket
Verbena bonariensis

PLANT A NECTAR-RICH WINDOWBOX FOR BUTTERFLIES

This is a quick and easy way to bring beautiful butterflies to your window, even if you live several storeys up. Bees will also pop by while the oregano is not only pretty but delicious on a pizza.

you will need

A large windowbox – about 60 cm long and 20 cm deep

Multipurpose peat-free compost

6 French marigold plants (*Tagetes patula*)

A lavender plant, such as Hidcote

An oregano or marjoram plant

when to do it

Spring to early summer

how to do it

Fill the windowbox almost to the top with compost. Plant the lavender and oregano plants in the middle of the box, then plant the marigolds around them in the remaining space. Water well and place in a sunny spot.

feed some very hungry caterpillars

The other way you can attract butterflies is by planting things their caterpillars eat. Anyone who grows cabbages or other brassicas knows how popular they are with large and small white butterflies – sometimes too much so. You don't have to sacrifice your lunch to bring in butterflies. Choose from the list, right.

a windowbox for caterpillars to munch

Encourage a new generation of beautiful butterflies by providing a food source for their young. Combine bird's foot trefoil, nasturtiums and wild strawberry in a windowbox or large container. The wild strawberry is attractive to the grizzled skipper and you can eat the fruits, too.

5 BEST FOOD PLANTS FOR CATERPILLARS

Garlic mustard attracts the orange tip

Nettles are a magnet for comma, red admiral, small tortoiseshell and peacock

Honeysuckle is fed on by white admiral

Bird's foot trefoil is fed on by, among others, clouded yellow, dingy skipper and common blue

Nasturtiums are beloved by large and small white butterflies (see Rurbanite: balcony wildlife gardener, page 94)

find

wild food ... wild flowers ... wildlife

Sometimes, we rurbanites are so busy trying to bring a bit of nature into the city by dashing around with a trowel that we forget to stop and notice the wildness already there.

As city people, we spend a lot of time walking pavements, waiting for buses and trains and gazing out of office windows. It can seem as though the world out there is sterile and grey. But, even in the most apparently inhospitable railway arches, skyscrapers, derelict factories and car parks, nature is doing its own thing. It's the dandelion weed growing in the crack of the concrete; it's the pigeons in a row on the tower block balcony, shifting up like old men in a queue for the bus.

Pausing to look, really look, at nature in the city is like unlocking the key to a whole new exciting language, whether you're in it for a free lunch or simply for the thrill of uncovering this treasure trove of plants, insects, birds and other animals going about their daily business under our noses.

FIND...WILD FOOD

Whenever we walk back from the shops

carrying our bagged salad leaves flown in from hundreds of miles away, we pass fresh wild food. Fruits and vegetables are growing in the parks, verges and at the roadside. There's more to urban foraging than blackberries, seductive as they are. If you know where to look you can supplement your diet year-round for free. You probably won't even get curious looks these days either. Urban foraging has become so popular in this time of thriftiness and food awareness that officials in Manhattan's Central Park recently had to stop people picking berries and leaves, afraid that they would end up with shrubbery stripped bare. Urban foraging is fun. You'll eat things you haven't tried, you'll explore areas of your city you never knew existed, all in the happy knowledge that you didn't have to open your wallet. Cities are great places for foraging since you are not restricted to the strictly native flora of the countryside's woods or meadows. Urban parks boast some exotic specimens, from figs to persimmons and ornamental quinces. Mahonia bushes, a favourite of municipal car parks, drip with purple berries that can be made into tangy syrup.

LEFT: A crack in the pavement is all this resourceful greater plantain plant needs to find a foothold.

RIGHT: City foraging in parks and other public areas can unearth some real treasures.

FORBIDDEN FRUIT?

'Fruit is a resource that should be commonly shared, like shells from the beach or mushrooms from the forest.' Fallen Fruit, Los Angeles

Whether it's growing on roadsides or in private gardens, a lot of fruit goes to waste in the city: apples, pears, cherries and plums are all left to fall on the ground and rot. Meanwhile, we spend money on fruit flown in from halfway across the world.

Lots of urbanites are on a mission to change this. In Seattle, Los Angeles, Toronto and London, harvesting groups have formed to pick unwanted city fruit. The Abundance movement, which started in Sheffield and has since spread to London and Manchester, involves volunteers and local schoolchildren who harvest fruit from gardens. They distribute it to the local community, turn it into jams, jellies or juice or sell it to restaurants on a non-profit basis. Last year, the London group picked 1.5 tonnes of fruit that would have ended up rotting on the ground.

In Los Angeles, a group of artists called Fallen Fruit map fruit trees accessible from the public highway and hold regular 'public fruit jams', where people arrive with fruit they've picked and throw it together to make weird and wonderful jams and jellies on the side of the road. Lemon-fig-lavender jam, anyone? Outraged at the lack of public fruit trees planted in their city, the group recently protested outside City Hall with placards proclaiming 'Fresh Fruit is a Human Right'.

Similar groups are being set up in cities all around the world – go on the internet and find a group near you (see Resources, page 168–169, for suggestions). Or why not pop a note through someone's letterbox if you see a fruit tree that looks like its harvest is going to waste. You could find yourself with a free bagful of quinces, figs or apples.

7

SPOTS FOR URBAN FORAGING

Parks
Allotments
Car parks
Roadsides
Churchyards
Waste ground
Canals or riversides

tip Even if branches from a fruit tree planted in a private garden are overhanging a public road, you should ask permission from the owner before picking.

urban foraging: before you start

1. Never eat anything you cannot identify with 100 per cent certainty. Some wild plants are poisonous so don't take any risks. If you have any doubt, cross check with a specialist guide (see Resources, page 168–169).
2. Pick only as much as you need and don't forget to leave some for the birds.
3. Don't pick in polluted places, such as near busy roads or where dogs may have been.

legal issues

1. Never uproot a wild plant, just pick the leaves and berries.
2. It's illegal to collect anything from a protected or rare plant.
3. You must get permission from the landowner to enter private land.
4. When foraging in public parks, ask an official before you pick: in most cases they are unlikely to object, though there are exceptions.

RURBANITE: Penny Greenhough, inner-city forager, Peckham

Peckham, south-east London, is not an area you normally associate with hedgerow harvests. The only blackberries you'd expect to find around these grey estates and alleyways are of the mobile phone variety. But Penny Greenhough sees it differently. She weaves through the neighbourhood following her own mental map, joining the dots between a loquat tree behind a local authority housing block, a mulberry tree in the Victorian park or a patch of wild raspberries behind a supermarket. Where passersby see only bland shrubbery, Penny sees potential for a jam, a jelly, rosehip or mahonia syrup (see Penny's Mahonia Syrup, page 126), mustard pickled quince, pickled walnuts and linden tea, jars of which fill her kitchen cupboards and shelves.

'When you find food for yourself the world feels safer.'

Penny gains a freedom through urban foraging, a way to opt out of the usual trade network of the large stores. 'It's working outside the money system. It makes you feel free,' she says. 'When you find food for yourself the world feels safer, more reliable – it rewards your resourcefulness.' A former midwife and aid worker who worked in a war zone during the Balkans conflict, Penny knows every centimetre of her neighbourhood and is passionate about defending the nature around her. When she saw people encouraging their dogs to bite into the trunk of a cherry tree on her street, she stood up for the tree and received a bruised jaw for her trouble.

This is a gritty part of town, but it's also full of growing treasure, much thanks to the Victorians who filled the public gardens with exotic specimens such as mulberry and fig trees, grapevines, loquats and persimmons. Penny knows every tree, bush and vine in Chumleigh Gardens, though she's not the only person with her eye on the mulberries. 'There's a community policeman who's very fond of them,' she says ruefully, 'and he's taller than I am.'

Penny's interest in connecting to her local land and what it produces is, she feels, symptomatic of a greater social mood change. 'In the 1980s no one talked to one another round here; there were riots, murders, the milkman wouldn't deliver,' she says. But now she's involved in a group setting up a garden in an abandoned part of a local park, where the community can grow vegetables in raised beds among the brambles. Looks like blackberries have a safe future in this part of town after all.

get your foraging eye in with these plants and berries, all of which are common sights in urban areas in parks, verges or gardens.

chickweed

This low-growing mat-like plant is a lovely wild green to eat in winter and early spring (avoid after that since it gets as stringy as an old vest). It has a round stem with a line of tiny hairs running down one side, small leaves which are rounded at the base and pointy at the top, and tiny white star-shaped flowers with five petals. Quite a few wild greens are bitter, but the young shoots of chickweed have a crunchy mildness not unlike lettuce or winter purslane. Shoots can also be cooked – when they do a very good impression of spinach – and are lovely with a knob of butter and a poached egg on toast. Once you start looking you'll see chickweed everywhere, in flowerbeds, planters, even in cracks in the pavement, so it's a good introduction for newbie foragers.

crab apples

Crab apples were once the classic trees of residential city streets in the 1970s and 1980s but their habit of growing actual fruit that might drop on someone's precious car has seen them fall from favour. This is a great shame, since they not only have extremely pretty blossom, but also delicious fruits that birds love and we can make into clear, ambrosial jelly for toast, crumpets and more. Look for a small tree with leaves the same shape as those of an edible apple tree and clusters of grape-sized fruits that can be any colour from yellow to red. You know it's a crab apple if cutting the fruit in half reveals a star shape with pips.

dandelions

The ubiquitous yellow pom-pom of sports pitches, mown grass and cracks in the pavement, the dandelion does more than brighten up lawns and provide an unreliable way for children to tell the time. The young leaves – really young, before the flowers appear – are good in salads with a crunchy, chicory-like bitterness that works well if mixed with milder leaves such as chickweed. You can also fry the young unopened buds with onion in butter. There are lots of other yellow pom-pom flowers around such as sow thistles (though these are edible too). You can tell it's a dandelion because it has a large single yellow flower on each hollow stem, and hairless, serrated or toothed leaves all in a rosette at the base.

goosegrass

Otherwise known as cleavers or sticky willy, in spring you notice this sprawling loose-limbed climber because it'll stick to your clothes when you pass by – the stems and narrow leaves have tiny hooks. It makes a good cooked vegetable if you pick only the very young spring shoots about 10cm in length. Boil or steam them and serve seasoned with butter.

hairy bittercress

This is often the first weed to pop up on bare soil in flowerbeds. It can survive the winter so is a great winter or early spring salad crop when there is little else about. Look for a basal cluster of small leaves topped by stems with lots of small white flowers. Despite its name, the leaves aren't particularly bitter, more like cabbage with a peppery-rocket kick. Pick the whole rosette before it flowers and eat raw with other salad leaves or wilt it into risottos.

mahonia

You may notice this large evergreen shrub – common in car parks, borders and street planters – when you pass it on a late winter's day and catch a fragrant waft of perfume from its yellow flowers, buzzing with bumblebees. You may also notice its clusters of grape-like purple fruits later in the summer (some forms are known as Oregon grape), which are a favourite with birds. You can tell when mahonia berries are ripe by the number of blackbirds eyeing you with suspicion. Wait until the whole cluster has turned from green to purple before picking.

how to MAKE STREET TREE JELLY

A mix of crab apples and rowan berries – both trees you're likely to find planted on an urban street – makes for a delicious jelly that's sweetly tangy rather than tart. It's great on toast or with meats such as lamb, duck or game.

you will need

500g rowan berries

500g crab apples

Granulated sugar

A jelly bag, muslin or clean pillowcase

1 hour

when to do it

Early to mid-autumn when the rowan berries are bright red and the crab apples come away easily from the tree (this indicates they are ripe)

how to do it

Wash the fruit and remove the stalks. Put it in a large, heavy-bottomed pan with enough water to just cover it. Bring to the boil and simmer, covered, for about 30 minutes until the mixture is soft. Mash it with a potato masher now and then to help break up the fruit. Tip into a large sieve (lined with the muslin) suspended over another large saucepan. Cover with a clean tea towel and leave overnight to drain. Don't squeeze the muslin or the jelly will be cloudy.

The next morning, measure how much juice you have, then add 750g of sugar to every litre of juice. Stir over a gentle heat until the sugar has dissolved then bring to the boil again. Skim off any froth that forms. Put a spoon in the fridge to chill then dip it into the jelly mixture. If, when it's cool, the surface of the jelly wrinkles when you touch it, it has reached setting point. If not, keep boiling and test a few minutes later. Once you are sure it has set, pour the jelly into sterilised jars.

how to make
PENNY'S MAHONIA SYRUP

You can eat mahonia berries raw – they taste a bit like blackberries – or dry them like currants to add to breakfast muesli. Another great way to preserve them is to turn them into this syrup, delicious drizzled on to pancakes or diluted with fizzy water for a refreshing summer drink. Use small bottles because the syrup doesn't keep for long once opened.

you will need

500g mahonia berries

Granulated sugar

A jelly bag or muslin

Small sterile bottles – clip top preserving bottles are ideal

A funnel

when to do

Mid to late-summer; the berries are ripe when the whole cluster has turned dark purple and they squish easily between your fingers, releasing red juice

how to do it

Remove your mahonia berries from their stalks with a fork into a bowl. Wash thoroughly and put in a pan with a small amount of water to prevent burning. Heat carefully, gently mashing and stirring as you go until the fruit has softened and yielded all its juices. Try not to boil. Strain carefully through a double layer of muslin or jelly bag.

Pour the strained juices back into a clean pan and, for each 0.5l juice, add 350g sugar. Heat gently, stirring until the sugar is dissolved. Skim if necessary and boil gently for a few minutes, then pour through the funnel into the sterile bottles and secure the lids. It will keep for a couple of months unopened. Refrigerate and use quickly once opened.

tip Make sure your funnel fits your bottles before you get to the filling stage.

rose

The hips of all roses are edible, but those of wild roses are best, with their cheery pink or white simple flowers, so unlike the multiple-petalled fuss of our garden roses. These hips tend to be fatter and more flavoursome and you'll find them at roadsides and in hedgerows, parks and on waste ground. The dog rose (*Rosa canina*) has pale pink (occasionally white) flowers and oval, pointy hips. The field rose (*Rosa arvensis*), which always has white flowers, has smaller, more rounded hips. The generous, wide hips of the immigrant Japanese rose (*Rosa rugosa*) with its fragrant dark pink flowers are so juicy you can eat them raw. They're also crying out to be made into jelly, cordial or syrup.

You can pick rosehips any time from early autumn to early winter, whenever they look red and ripe. Avoid any that are bruised or marked. They are surprisingly easy to harvest though you may need gloves to avoid the thorns on the stems – simply twist the hip off at the stem and it will break off with a satisfying snap.

how to make
A MUG OF ROSEHIP TEA

All rosehips make a fine tea, high in Vitamin C and antioxidants. You can make it from fresh or dried hips. Sweetened with a little honey, or a dash of orange juice and sugar, it is a real virus buster, and there's something deeply satisfying about how quickly the bullet-hard fruits can be transformed to a beautiful orangey-pink, healthy brew.

you will need

About 6 fresh ripe rosehips

Boiling water

A sharp knife

20 minutes

when to do it

Early autumn to early winter

how to do it

Wash the hips then cut them in half with a sharp knife. Dig out the seed and irritating fine hairs. Wash well to remove any last traces of hair. Then chop up and place at the bottom of a cup. Pour on boiling water and steep for 10 minutes. Sweeten to taste with honey or sugar. You can also use dried rose hips for a stronger flavour. Wash and chop the ends off the hips, then dry them until they are hard. Chop them up in a food processor then sieve to remove the white hairs. Put the mixture in an airtight jar and place in an airtight jar. Add two tablespoons to a teapot and strain before drinking.

rowan

Rowan, otherwise known as mountain ash, is often planted as a street tree in cities since it won't grow too tall, has lovely white blossom in the spring and beautiful red berries in autumn beloved by birds. Why not get into the action and harvest some yourself for delicious jelly (see How to Make Street Tree Jelly, page 125)? You might need to borrow a chair from a nearby shop though since street tree branches tend to be rather high. Rowans can also be found in hedgerows and parks. Look for medium-sized trees with dark green pinnate leaves (each leaf having a row of narrow pointed leaflets on either side of the midrib), though you'll probably notice the profusion of red berries first.

smooth sow thistle

With their fluffy yellow flowers and serrated leaves, these can be mistaken for dandelions. But their leaves grow all the way up the stem rather than just in a rosette at the base of the plant. Also the flowers are smaller than those of dandelions, and you'll get more than one on each stem. The classic urban survivor, this will grow anywhere, from waste ground to tree pits and pavements. When young in the spring, before flowering, cut the whole rosette just above the root with scissors or a knife – it makes a delicious steamed vegetable rather like chard. The raw leaves, which taste a bit like lettuce, are an important part of the Italian dish Insalata di Campo, or field salad. The Maoris of New Zealand cook the leaves and eat them with fish.

stinging nettles

There's nothing like being stung to sharpen your identification skills. From childhood onwards most of us can recognise this hairy plant at twenty paces with its serrated, heart-shaped leaves. Look for clumps of nettles in churchyards, waste ground, gardens and verges. The best time to pick them for eating is spring before they start flowering, though you'll find new plants shooting in late summer too. Wearing gloves, snip off the tops, about six leaves' worth. Make tea with four or five nettle leaves, eat them steamed as a vegetable, as a filling for ravioli or use them to make pesto. But the traditional way to cook them is in a soup.

how to MAKE NETTLE SOUP

There's something particularly satisfying about turning something that can hurt you into a delicious meal. Stinging nettles are full of vitamins and iron and make a hearty soup with an earthy taste somewhere between spinach and cabbage, but richer than both. Look for clumps of nettles out of the way of potential motor or dog traffic and don't forget to wear gloves.

you will need

Half a carrier bag of stinging nettle tops, the top four to six leaves

50g butter

2 onions, peeled and finely chopped

1 large potato, peeled and cubed

1l vegetable stock

2 tablespoons of double cream

Scissors or secateurs

30 minutes

when to do it

Springtime, before they flower. Alternatively, late summer, when there is a burst of new growth. Old, stringy plants are best avoided.

how to do it

Wash the nettles thoroughly in hot water (this removes their sting). Melt the butter in a heavy-bottomed saucepan then add the onions and let them cook for 5 minutes on a gentle heat. Add the potato cubes and stir-fry until they begin to soften. Then add the nettles. Cook for another minute then add the stock. Simmer for 5 minutes then blend it smooth with a hand stick blender. Season, pour into bowls and add a dollop of cream at the last moment. Serve with warm, crusty bread.

LEFT: Stinging nettles thrive on any disturbed land, but avoid those too close to pathways if picking to eat.

Foraging is fun, but plants and animals

don't need to be edible to be interesting. There is a real pleasure in getting to know your wild neighbours out and about in the city, in places you might not expect. More and more young people are becoming passionate about urban ecology as the need to preserve native flora and fauna becomes ever more pressing. And it's a passion that technology has revolutionised. They are taking photos of insects or flowers they pass on their way to work and posting them on Twitter or in internet forums for instant identification.

You no longer have to leaf through endless specialist books to identify that strange-looking caterpillar – you can just snap it on your iPhone and Google it when you get back to your computer. Websites such as iSpot – in which you post an image and await an identification from like-minded amateurs anywhere in the world – are uniting people who have a passion for urban ecology, many of whom still have their own teeth and don't wear socks under their sandals.

There is, of course, a wealth of insects, fungi, amphibians and small mammals out there, some more elusive to the rurban spotter than others. It's impossible to cover every creature so we'll put the focus on two easy groups, both true rurbanites who have adapted to city life: wildflowers and birds. You'll spot these every day even on a five-minute trip to the corner shop.

RIGHT: Frogs can thrive in cities as long as they have access to shelter and a pond.

FAR RIGHT: Swathes of ox-eye daisies and buttercups cheer up the verge of a busy road.

FIND... URBAN WILDFLOWERS

It's impossible not to admire the opportunism of wildflowers in cities.

Plants are nothing if not resourceful. They turn ugly run-down places into beautiful ones, wallpapering over the cracks with ivy, blood-red poppies, tenacious buddleia or a swathe of ox-eye daisies. Wildflowers don't ask permission or demand any effort from us, and they seem all the more beautiful for it.

Cities are perfect for wildflowers. Many like low-fertility, free-draining habitats, so rubble and thin, dusty soils on former industrial sites or waste ground are ideal. These soils are not only low in nutrients, but dry too, and drought-stressed plants tend to flower more intensely. The digger is their friend too. Many wildflowers thrive in disturbed landscapes, their long-dormant seed sparked into life when brought to the surface by construction work. It's no coincidence that the number of wildflowers quadrupled in the city of London from the beginning to the end of the Second World War. They liked the rubble of the bombsites. Carpets of rosebay willowherb were soon seen throughout war-torn European cities damaged by bombing, the plant soon gained the nickname 'bombweed' in the UK.

Constant human traffic in cities makes for some interesting wildflower arrivals. Seed goes where people go – trains returning from the seaside mean coastal plants often appear around inland rail stations, from seed that fell off day-trippers' shoes. Buddleia arrived in England from China as a garden plant in Victorian times and soon escaped up the rail tracks thanks to the air current of moving trains. Its native habitat of cliff faces was not so different from the brick bridges and embankments. Although it attracts butterflies, it also shades out caterpillar food plants and is now considered an invasive weed in Europe and much of the USA.

It's impossible not to admire the opportunism of wildflowers in cities. They escape from front gardens, creeping down the pavement from house to house. Some will take advantage of any chip in the tarmac or crevice in a wall to embed their roots, each year dislodging more man-made material to make a more comfortable home. This opportunism can inspire us. In Manhattan, an abandoned aerial section of the New York Central Railroad became filled with tree of heaven seedlings, goldenrod, wild carrot and evening primrose. It so delighted the city residents that they turned it into a park: the High Line is now a beautiful ribbon high above the traffic along which people can walk among the waving grasses and flowers. A similar project is now planned for a disused aerial rail track in east London.

Not all 'weed' incursions have such harmonious outcomes. Wildflower imports can cause havoc since the pests and diseases that keep them in check in their

BELOW: Oppurtunistic teasels find their way into a London garden.

ABOVE: Wild flowers growing on a disused stretch of rail track in Manhattan inspired residents to turn it into a celebrated public park, the High Line.

native country are not necessarily present in their new one. Japanese knotweed (*Fallopia japonica*), imported into British woodland gardens in the Victorian age has now become so invasive it is categorised by the government as a noxious weed. Its shoots can lift concrete slabs. Clearing it from the Olympic site in London cost £70 million since it had to be buried 5 metres below ground to ensure it wouldn't reappear. The kudzu vine (*Pueraria lobata*) was introduced as a garden ornamental from Asia to the USA in the 1870s, since when it has gone rampant: its ability to grow 30cm in 12 hours means it can smother whole buildings. Cogon grass (*Imperata cylindrica*) thrived in the forests of Vietnam after defoliation by Agent Orange by US troops. It has now been imported in packaging into the USA from Asia and is taking over natural habitats.

In really built-up urban areas, wildflowers remind us that, however unnatural our environment, nature is never far away. In her project 'Tagworts', British artist Sue Lawes celebrated this by roaming the pavements and car parks of Deptford, south-east London, 'tagging' common wildflowers such as dandelions and groundsel with bold yellow stencils on the pavement. An accompanying online map showed where you could find each specimen. Her aim was to embrace 'weeds' into the city. It certainly made them hard to miss.

Wild vegetation is not only around us in the city, it's trying to gain ground. According to Alan Weisman's book *The World Without Us*, if human beings were to be wiped out tomorrow, a human house would be nothing but a 'swelling in the ground' within 50 years, a mound covered with trees. It's an alarming and comforting thought, depending on your frame of mind.

Once you start noticing the wildflowers in your neighbourhood, a switch is turned on. You'll see beauty in even the most common ones. You'll start wanting to identify them, crouching on the pavement with your camera phone and getting curious looks from passersby. In some cases, you might even want to eat them (see Find Wild Food, page 121). If nothing else, knowing your groundsels from your chickweed, and your greater celandine from your sow thistles will make a walk around the block a whole lot more interesting.

ABOVE: Buddleia came to Europe from China in Victorian times and swiftly colonised railway embankments.

LEFT: Blood-red poppies create a profusion of colour on this roadside.

BELOW: A thistle in full flower enlivens an urban heath.

what flower am I looking at?

Look closely. And then look even more closely than you thought could be humanly necessary. That's the basic rule of wildflower identification. It's illegal in the UK and in many states in the USA to uproot any wildflower without permission from the landowner. This can be a bit of a grey area – since even 'public' land is generally owned – so it's best to avoid uprooting any wild plant. It's amazing how hard it is to remember what a plant actually looks like after you've taken leave of it. Did it have pointy leaves? Were there five petals? Were the sepals long or short? Um, can't remember. Take a photo on your phone or make a quick sketch.

Even the most nascent of interests in wildflowers will introduce you swiftly to Latin names and botanical terms you previously had only a dim understanding of. Forget petals, stems and leaves, we're talking 'bracts', 'sepals' and 'inflorescences'. All this can be intimidating at first, but soon becomes familiar. Noticing the shape and arrangement of the leaves and the smoothness or otherwise of the stems will soon become second nature. When so many plants look alike, these little details may be all there is to tell them apart.

Don't be afraid of Latin names – some are quite helpful. For example, *stellata* means star-shaped; *dentata* means toothed and *viscosus* means sticky.

5 best places to find wildflowers in the city

Out of the car, bus or train window
The verges of roads can be a good hunting ground for wildflowers, even in built-up areas. Train embankments and sidings provide particularly rich pickings because they are undisturbed by human traffic; you might see sprawling wild roses, swathes of ox-eye daisies, goldenrod, common mallow and rosebay willowherb. The draught of the train also means seed spreads quickly along the track and the chippings on which track is laid make a nice free-draining seedbed. Look out for dandelions (see page 124), smooth and prickly sow thistle (see page 128), ragwort, Michaelmas daisies, goosegrass (see page 124), groundsel, nipplewort, valerian and buddleia.

Closely mown grass
When you walk across a sports pitch or park it can seem at first glance to be a desert for wildflowers, but look more closely and you'll find it's a patchwork of all sorts of gems. Daisies, dandelions, plantains, hawkbits, buttercups, clovers and catsears all thrive in mown grass, since they have evolved from grazing plants for livestock. They're used to a severe haircut. Purple-flowered ground ivy, self-heal, bird's foot trefoil and bugle are other common lawn plants and in early spring you might even see violets. Many of these plants are magnets to bees.

Pavements
It's awe-inspiring how plants can just sprout from the tiniest crack in a pavement or foot of a wall. Many will flower and set seed fast since their roots are so stressed.

Walk down any city street and chances are you'll spot dandelions, sow thistles, plantains, prickly lettuce, hairy bittercress (see page 124), annual mercury, shepherd's purse and chickweed (see page 124).

Beyond chainlink fencing at an abandoned site
This is the type of site where wildflowers can get into their stride. Expect armies of brambles, cow parsley, nettles (see page 128) and buddleia. The ability of tree of heaven seedlings, which are native to Asia, to sprout in pavement cracks in New York is so legendary that it inspired *A Tree Grows in Brooklyn*, a famous 1943 book about immigration to the USA.

Rosebay willowherb and goldenrod are other quick colonisers of waste ground. Other plants that thrive in poor soils might turn up too such as valerian, bindweed, common mallow, goosegrass and greater celandine.

Looking up
Some plants just pop out from cracks in walls, defying gravity. Look out for buddleia and valerian launching themselves bravely. Other likely wall huggers include ivy-leaved toadflax, pellitory-of-the-wall and ivy, a haven for birds nesting in its tangles or eating its black berries over winter when there is not much else around.

LEFT: Road verges and railway embankments are particularly rich in city wild flowers because they are undisturbed by human traffic.

ABOVE RIGHT: A wild clematis effortlessly scales a chainlink fence on a brownfield site.

5
· · · · · ·
EASY TO COLLECT WILDFLOWER SEEDS

Knapweed
Poppies
Teasel
Thistles
Viper's bugloss

tip
By the time the seed of wildflowers is ripe, the defining flowers will be long gone so it might be difficult to identify them. Get used to making a mental note of likely plants earlier in the season so you can return to them later with confidence.

Can I collect wildflower seed?

In the UK, as long as you choose common varieties and only take a small quantity of seed for personal use (remember, uprooting plants is illegal), there is no harm in collecting seed from wildflowers growing in public areas near you. Check with the wildflower associations of your country to be sure of local legislation. Scatter seed in your garden at home or in bare tree pits, roundabouts or other neglected public planted areas to increase your local biodiversity. Here are some of the easiest, common wildflowers to save seed from... (see also How to Collect and Save Seed, page 63).

identifying wildflowers: some tips

1. Use all your senses: smell and crush the leaves. Run the leaves and stem through your fingers, are they smooth or hairy? What colour is the sap? Do the leaves have a fragrance? Bear in mind that the leaves might differ in shape depending on where they are on the stem.
2. Take close-up photos of the plant on your phone or a camera so you can identify it with books or in internet sites at home.
3. Although you can't uproot a plant, taking a single leaf to look at more closely at home won't do a plant any harm. Put it in a plastic bag to stop it wilting.
4. Examine the leaves, stem and flowers closely. What shape are the leaves and how are they arranged on the stem? Are they in opposite pairs or staggered up the stem? Count the petals on the flowers. Is the stem solid or hollow, round or ridged?
5. Find a patch local to you that you look at closely – a street on your way to work, for example. If you get to know an area in detail you'll notice when something new and exciting turns up.

LEFT: The stunning blue flowers of viper's bugloss are a magnet for bumble bees and butterflies.

MEET... URBAN BIRDS

Whether they're circling like distant dots high in the sky or pecking at last night's takeaway in a park bin, birds are everywhere in our cities.

We can all identify a pigeon or the cheeky stance of a robin. But there is more to these feathered creatures than the brief glimpse they show us as they dash past the window.

You'd think living in a busy city would be pretty unappealing for a bird. But there are compensations. Most cities contain green 'island' areas and these can attract surprisingly dense numbers of bird species, while the urban heat island effect (see page 105) can make for a comfortable life. Research has recently suggested that urban birds get up later than country birds, the relative warmth of their nights meaning they don't have to eat so early to replace energy reserves.

Tall skyscrapers can do a good impression of cliffs. Peregrine falcons and kestrels are often seen in London, Chicago and Manhattan, circling the tops of the towers and nesting high up in peace. Feral pigeons are another happy city dweller, finding railways, arches, bridges and other concrete structures a good stand-in for the cliff faces their rock dove ancestors enjoyed in the wild. They're considered so numerous in London that locals call them 'rats with wings', although their numbers in the city are actually in decline, thanks to spikes erected to stop them roosting and the release of sparrowhawks into train and underground stations to scare them away. In Moscow, it's hooded crows that have made

themselves too much at home for city officials: trained falcons are now regularly released to stop them sliding down the onion domes, scratching the gold leaf. In the Coliseum in the heart of Rome, falcons are released to deter the crowds of blackbirds, ravens and seagulls which nest and peck for seed in the crannies, dislodging masonry that could fall on tourists.

Urban birds have to adapt to live in our cities – and what it tells us about the way we live isn't always pleasant. Dutch researchers have discovered that male birds in built-up urban areas have to sing in a higher key to try to compete with noise pollution from low-rumbling traffic, aeroplanes and industry. Urban crows studied in Vienna have been found to differentiate between familiar and unfamiliar human voices, a talent that could help them identify potential threats in a city environment. Migratory birds aren't such city slickers – lured and disoriented by the lights of skyscrapers, about 6.8 million of them are killed each year in collisions with buildings in the USA and Canada alone. The cities of Chicago and Toronto now have strong campaigns encouraging office workers to turn off the lights when they leave for the night.

Not all birds like living in built-up areas but many (known as 'urban adapter' species) do, happily nesting in man-made sites, from the wheel arches of cars to hanging baskets, air-conditioning vents, traffic lights and street lamps (see box on page 141). They seem to be able to cope with noise, artificial light and pollution astonishingly well. These 'urban adapter' species tend to have big brains relative to their body size. Seems like you really do have to be streetwise to live in the city.

RURBANITE: David Lindo, urban birder, London

When David Lindo gets off the plane in a foreign city, his first port of call isn't the hotel, but the local rubbish tip, wasteland or park. He is used to the curious looks of taxi drivers, but these are water off a duck's back in his mission to spread the word about urban birds.

'Just because we don't think an area looks nice, doesn't mean birds see it in the same way. One of the best places I ever went birding was in Addis Ababa in Ethiopia. Behind the hotel right in the middle of town was a building site. It stank to high heaven because people used it as a public latrine. There were flies everywhere. But in four days I saw about sixty species.' Every morning David patrols his beloved patch of London's Wormwood Scrubs – home to a prison, a hospital, factories, a depot for the Channel Tunnel – and a whole lot of his feathered friends.

'See the city as the birds see it, view the buildings as craggy lumps of rock.'

'People have this thing that the only birds in cities are pigeons,' he says, 'but anything can turn up at any time. When birding in a city, try to see the world as a bird would see it. Ignore the people and view the buildings as craggy lumps of rock; that's urban birding. To birds, brambles on a city roundabout are no different to those on remote islands; they just see them as a food source. Birds exploit nesting sites: to them nesting in a hole, in a building, or in a kettle is the same as nesting in a cliff.'

For Lindo, understanding urban birds is a way to get people to connect with wildlife in general. 'Eighty per cent of people in the UK live in the city,' he says, 'and they're disconnected from nature because the only wildlife they see on TV is in the countryside. If they had any awareness they wouldn't rip up their hedgerow in the back garden.'

10 tips for urban birding

1. Get to know a patch well and really love it. You'll soon notice variations or unusual things turning up.

2. Get some binoculars with reasonable magnification (x7 or x8 is ideal for beginners) and a comfortable strap.

3. Buy a good field guide and download a decent bird identification app (see Resources, page 168–169, for suggestions).

4. Practise spotting birds with binoculars by tracking slow-moving objects like aeroplanes through the sky.

5. Look for movement in the trees or overhead and then bring your binoculars to your eyes rather than trying to find birds through your binoculars.

6. Don't get obsessed with identifying every species you see. Just enjoy watching the birds and getting to know them. Species knowledge will come naturally later.

7. A great way to get to know the birds around you is to get to know their songs first. The internet is full of sites with audio clips of various bird songs and calls. Download an app on your phone and listen to it when you're out and about for an instant match.

8. Start birding in the morning when birds are out looking for food.

9. Don't just look at tree height, look straight up for birds of prey such as peregrine falcons, buzzards and kestrels. You might also catch a glimpse of migrating birds passing high overhead.

10. Keep quiet and put your phone on vibrate.

Why is London so full of ring-necked parakeets?
The UK now boasts around 31,000 of these noisy, exotic birds, most around London and the South East. How did these Himalayan natives get here? Take your pick…

urban myth 1: In the 1960s Jimi Hendrix let loose a couple of parakeets on Carnaby Street in London. Could these be their descendants?

urban myth 2: They escaped in 1951 from Isleworth Studios during filming of *The African Queen* starring Humphrey Bogart and Katharine Hepburn.

5 best places to see urban birds

Gardens and parks
With their combinations of trees, hedges, lawns and ponds, city gardens are ideal bird habitats. Look out for robins, blackbirds, tits, thrushes, crows, woodpeckers, wrens, house sparrows and hedge sparrows or dunnocks. During the summer you might see swifts and swallows.

Commons and sports pitches
Thrushes, starlings, finches and crows are the most likely birds you'll see here, searching for seeds, insects and worms. During winter, loafing gulls might join them.

Derelict sites and waste ground
These are popular sites for many birds from feral pigeons to thrushes, house sparrows, starlings, black redstarts and finches. The rough grass and brambles of waste ground is an ideal bird habitat in cities: dunnocks, wrens, black caps, whitethroats, chiff chaffs, blackbirds, woodcocks and even nightingales can sometimes be seen in these areas.

Tower blocks
Watch for birds flying past such as cormorants, gulls, ducks, geese, peregrine falcons and other birds of prey. Birds are attracted to lights and birds of prey hunt by them. At one point the beacon on top of the skyscraper in London Docklands, 1 Canada Square, was the brightest spot in northern Europe. Soon the small gardens around the area were full of unusual birds.

tip To encourage birds into your garden, hang up nesting boxes and bird feeders (see page 140); and grow plants with berries or seedheads that they particularly like (see page 114). A container pond will be a welcome bath and drink spot for them too (see Make a Wildlife Pond in a Pot, page 96).

how to make
A WINDOW BIRD FEEDER

Even if you live in a flat and have no balcony or windowsills, you can still get close to birds if you make a feeder that attaches to the windowpane. It's all made from materials you might already have in the house or can easily find in a homeware store. It might take a few weeks for the birds to get used to the feeder, but once they do, you should have plenty flocking to your armchair hide. Placing it on a window near existing greenery will make them feel more secure.

you will need

A clear 1l plastic bottle (with the lid screwed on)

Scissors

2 plastic suction cups with s-hooks

Electrical or duct tape

Bird seed

String (optional)

Vinegar

Cloth

20 minutes

when to do it

Any time of year

how to do it

Turn the plastic bottle on its side and cut out a central panel about 5cm high along almost the entire length. Seal the edges with duct tape so they are smooth. Then make two small holes in the other side of the bottle with sharp scissors, one at each end. Push the s-hooks into the holes. Turn the bottle back on its side and fill with seed up to the opening. To attach it securely to the window, first clean the glass with a mixture of vinegar and water. Soak the suction cups in warm water for five minutes to make them pliable then reattach them to the feeder and stick it to the window.

ABOVE: A nuthatch, American goldfinch and greenfinches flock to feeders hung up in a city garden.

RIGHT: House sparrows have lived intimately with humans in cities for centuries.

Very built-up areas

Feral pigeons, peregrines, house sparrows and starlings can often be spotted in areas close to human activity. Pied wagtails have been known to roost right next to shopping centres, attracted to the warmth. A family of thrushes in Leeds city centre has been snapped living inside a traffic light at a busy junction, seemingly unbothered by the stream of traffic a few feet below.

tip You might like to tie a length of string tightly around the lid end. This can be tied to the window handle so that, if the suction cups don't hold at first, the bottle won't fall on the heads of people below!

7 TOP 'URBAN ADAPTER' BIRDS

Blue tits
Great tits
Long-tailed tits
Carrion crows
Magpies
Nuthatches
Wrens

keep

Keeping hens, quails and ducks
Keeping bees

You may not secretly want to herd a flock of sheep over London Bridge or milk goats on the Champs-Elysee, but the chances are that if you're a true rurbanite your dreams will, at the very least, be full of clucking chickens and humming beehives. After all, why stop at growing potatoes when you could be producing eggs to go with them, and honey for your toast?

Any livestock is a responsibility, so don't rush into buying, and do check your local regulations first (in some cities, keeping 'farm animals' is illegal). Larger farm animals such as pigs, cows and sheep are not a realistic option in the city, but the average urban garden can be a happy home for a beehive, a handful of hens, some quail or even a couple of ducks. Even a balcony could provide the right conditions for a beehive or some quail. The birds will fertilise your soil, eat weeds and slugs, provide delicous eggs and grow into surprisingly companionable pets. Just be prepared to butter an awful lot of soldiers.

A city garden can be great place for a few hens and they really are, as one London henkeeper calls them, 'pets with benefits'. Not only will they provide you with fresh, delicious eggs, but also hours of entertainment. Anyone who keeps hens finds their birds endlessly fascinating – they're friendly and inquisitive and will follow you around when you do the weeding. As long as you provide them with the right accommodation and food, hens are no more bother than a cat or dog. And then there's the golden bonus. Three hens could supply you with fresh eggs all year.

There are now estimated to be 700,000 back-garden hens in Britain, the biggest revival in henkeeping since the Second World War. And some of them don't even have their chicken feet on the ground. Farm:Shop in Dalston, east London, might look like any other small shop from the outside, but this urban farming 'hub' has a polytunnel in the back garden, fish swimming around tanks in a mini aquaculture operation in the café inside and hydroponic tomatoes in a foil-wrapped room. The crowning attraction, though, is on the roof where three hens scratch contentedly around in a coop overlooking a busy road. 'They're very happy,' says Farm:Shop founder Andy Merritt, 'and there are no foxes.' They are by no means the only urban roof hens. Across the Atlantic in their long run on a rooftop in Brooklyn, the hens of Eagle Street Rooftop Farm have an even better view – the Empire State Building.

Of course, hens have lived alongside humans in cities for hundreds of years. They still do in much of the developing world, most roaming free. In the UK, up to and especially during the Second World War it was considered normal to keep a few hens in the back garden, but after the war, egg production moved inside, inevitably towards battery farming.

These days keeping hens in cities such as New York and London is not about economic necessity. Eggs are cheap to buy, after all, and – unless you are a particularly dab hand with a hammer and saw – henhouses are not, even if you can now buy them along with your muesli from the major high-street supermarkets. But, rather like growing your own food, keeping hens in a city garden appeals to us because it's a way to connect to the natural world and to the food production process and it signals our discomfort at some of its methods. The fact that battery hens live in a space the size of an A4 piece of paper is so shocking that people have taken matters into their own hands. The British Hen Welfare Trust has seen its annual number of re-homings for battery chickens rise from 5,000 in 2004 to a clucking 60,000 in 2011.

It is true that pressure on the commercial egg industry has had an impact. The European Union banned battery hen production in 2012 and moved towards 'enriched' cages, which allow the hens a place to roost, perch, scratch and dust bathe. The egg industry in the USA is likely to follow suit. But several EU member states haven't signed up to the ban and, even if they did, the enriched system has its critics. These hens still have no access to daylight or enough room to stretch their wings.

This is all the more reason to rear hens at home and collect guilt-free, happy eggs in the morning. The free entertainment is a bonus – hens are friendly, docile and look funny when they walk.

'Honestly, these chickens give you a lot. Besides the eggs, they're hilarious. Name them for folks you know and you'll never be bored.'
@BetteMidler, Twitter, March 2012

5 reasons to keep hens in the city

1 They'll give you delicious, healthy fresh eggs. Most 'fresh' eggs you buy in the supermarket are three weeks old.

2 They're hilarious to watch and you can have fun naming them. Old-fashioned titles are popular, with Henrietta (naturally), Daisy, Mabel, Bella and Ruby coming top in a recent customer internet survey by the henhouse company, Omlet. Puns are favourites too: anyone for Attila the Hen, Yolko and Sam and Ella?

3 If you eat eggs laid by happy home-reared hens, you are doing your bit for animal welfare.

4 They'll eat your slugs and snails (and, unfortunately your salads, cabbages and tomatoes, see page 152) and their droppings, super-high in nitrogen, phosphates and potash, will work wonders in your compost heap. Don't add fresh droppings to your plants though or they will scorch them.

5 It's not expensive: once you've set them up, the cost of feeding and housing a bird can work out at as little as 3–5 pence a day, or around £14 a year.

not-so-fantastic mr fox

While rural hens seem to get off lightly – at least in daylight hours – poor old urban hens have a horrible time with foxes, who will apply themselves to seeking out and killing your feathered friends with a *Shawshank Redemption*-style commitment. It's not unusual for an owner to find a run full of dead chickens and a tiny hole in the chicken wire, evidence of a fox's patient gnawing over several nights.

The only way to deter foxes is to buy a really good-quality fox-proof henhouse and keep your hens firmly locked in at night. Never let your hens roam free in the garden unless you are there. It's been known for someone to pop in and put the kettle on, to return five minutes later and find a garden of ghoulish feathers.

so you want to keep hens...

Can I just buy my hens over the internet?

It's best to get local recommendations from other hen keepers, but if none are forthcoming, look on the internet for suppliers near you, and make a point of visiting to see the hens before you buy. This way you can see how healthy the hens are and what conditions they have been raised in. Ideally, buy vaccinated hens.

I know nothing about hens, how do I begin?

It's a good idea to spend some time with some hens before you commit to the idea, just to make sure you feel comfortable handling them (some people find they aren't). If you don't know anyone who already keeps hens, join your local henkeeping association for help.

Do I have time for hens?

Like any pet, hens need attention, but no more so than a cat. Expect to spend about 10 minutes on them each day. In the morning you'll feed them, collect eggs and remove dirty bedding. In the evening, you'll feed them again and shut them up for the night. Once a week give the henhouse a clean, with a thorough going over every two months to deep clean and remove cobwebs.

How many hens should I get?

If you're a beginner with an average-sized city garden and average-sized egg consumption, two or three bantams are ideal. The bonsais of the chicken world, these are about a quarter of the size of a traditional chicken and tame easily. They will also be less destructive on your garden plants. You can expect each bantam hen to lay approximately 200 eggs a year, depending on breed. Bear in mind that most are pure-breeds which means that they tend to stop laying over winter (hybrid chickens will lay eggs more frequently and year-round too, but tend to be bigger and take a greater toll on your garden). Though hens can live for a dozen years, all will lay progressively fewer eggs after their first year of laying.

5 things you might not know about hens

1. American consumers prefer to buy white eggs, Brits brown eggs. There is no difference to the egg within the shell.

2. Hen or chicken, is there a difference? A hen is a female chicken; a cockerel is a male chicken.

3. Hens can't see in the dark so will always make their own way to bed before dusk.

4. Hens do two-thirds of their droppings at night.

5. Araucana hens from Chile lay blue eggs.

5 top city cluckers

Choose from some of these pint-sized layers, all happy to live in the city. Remember when cooking, you'll need three bantam eggs for every two standard eggs.

Buff Orpington bantam
Docile and maternal, this pure-breed is extremely friendly and cuddly looking. Its thick feathers make it very hardy in the cold. It lays large, tinted eggs.

Sussex bantam
Plump, hardy and friendly, this pure-breed bird has a distinctive black and white colouring. It lays lovely tinted eggs. It loves a treat and has a curious nature so will make a good gardening companion as well as a good pet for children.

Pekin (known as cochin bantams in the US)
A perfect beginner-bird, this gentle pure-breed has feathery feet and short legs and only comes in bantam size. Its feathery feet mean it doesn't like scratching through flowerbeds so your vegetables may be safer, but its feathers can become caked with mud when damp. It lays lovely small brown eggs though expect productivity to drop off after the first year.

Wyandotte bantam
These perky-looking birds from the USA have broad breasts and a distinctive curvy shape. A pure-breed, birds are docile and some have very pretty feather patterns. Good layers.

Rhode Island Red bantam
Perhaps the most popular hen in the world, this US breed is the classic traditional-looking red hen and lays lots of large traditional-looking brown eggs. A quiet, alert bird with an endearing nature: it loves foraging and eating slugs.

where will my hens live?

All you need is a watertight structure with adequate ventilation, somewhere for the hens to perch and somewhere for them to lay their eggs. You can convert a playhouse (see page 150), dog kennel, garden shed or even an old wardrobe, but most city henkeeping beginners plump for a shop-bought house. The best are raised off the ground to deter rats and mice nesting underneath. Whether you go for plastic or wood, prices will be around the same. Avoid houses with felt roofs since they can harbour red mite, a nasty parasite. A plastic one is easy to clean and maintain. Simply hose the whole thing down and it will dry quickly. Its bright colours and distinctive styling also gives it a distinctly 21st century look. A wooden house blends in a little better in a garden, but will take a lot longer to dry.

I have a small garden

In a small city garden you have two options. The first is to buy a henhouse with an attached run that is small and light enough to move to a new spot in the garden every week to let the grass recover. An Eglu, henhouse on wheels, or a traditional wooden ark is ideal for this (see Resources, page 168–169).

The alternative is to buy a raised henhouse within a head-height run and put it in a permanent position. This is ideal since it is easy to clean and the hens have lots of space and different levels to explore. If this is too expensive, you can also build a large full-time run at the end of the garden and put the henhouse inside it.

Whatever set-up you go for, make sure the run is big enough for each hen to have at least 1 square metre to run around in, and preferably a lot more.

free-range hens: a henhouse and run you can move

Pros No DIY needed.
Cons Your grass will take a beating, you'll have to remember to move it and this is usually a two-person operation. Not so much space for the hens to roam unless you let them out now and then. Most city lawns are small so there might not be enough time for each patch of grass to recover.

home-run hens: a static run

Pros Runs can give hens more room and are easier to clean too. If you build it yourself, the run will only cost the price of some wooden posts and weld wire. Your lawn will stay undamaged unless you let them out. You can store their food in a secure dustbin inside the run so won't have to carry it down the garden.
Cons The larger the run, the more expensive it is. Building your own run can be challenging if you are not a DIY enthusiast. The floor of the run will get muddy fast although bark chippings can easily be laid on the floor to absorb it.

how do I build a run?

Make the run out of 6-foot wooden posts with weld mesh for the walls and roof. Bring the base of the netting out into an apron where it meets the ground and secure this with paving slabs or turf to stop foxes getting in. If you don't want to build a run, try customizing a fruit cage. Just replace the netting with weld mesh. An internet search will turn up plenty of tutorials on how to build a hen run (see Resources, page 168–170, for suggestions).

RURBANITE: Olivia, Laurie, Vera-Lily and Emmanuel, henkeepers, London

Olivia and her husband Laurie are eating bacon and eggs while an inquisitive ex-battery hen is eyeballing them through the kitchen door. Perhaps she wants to know where her eggs end up. 'I don't understand why people would have a garden and not keep chickens,' says Olivia. Laurie, polishing off the last of his egg on toast, agrees: 'They're pets with benefits.'

Every morning they collect eggs from their seven hens – a collection of bantams, hybrids and ex-battery layers who call this 24m-long, south-London garden home. The average yield is an egg per hen per day, all year round. They and their two children, Vera-Lily and Emmanuel, eat a lot of eggs, and they give a lot away too. 'We hand them across the fence to our Jamaican neighbour who gives us jerk chicken in return.'

During the winter, the hens Millie, Flower, Molly, Jake, Henry, Merrylegs and Miss Pepperpot are free to roam the garden all day, pecking at woodlice and worms, stalking the beds and taking their chances with Mr Fox who makes occasional appearances and has had to be chased from the garden by Olivia in bare feet. From spring into summer, Olivia's precious vegetable beds take precedence and the

'Hens are a commitment, but it's fun. Like playing farm.'

hens are kept in a roomy run at the back of the garden in which she parks a chair and sits staring in fascination at their behaviour. 'My husband looks out the window and shouts: "You look like my mad wife in a cage".'

A former brand director in the city, Olivia has been keeping hens for about four years. The garden is a hymn to resourcefulness. No pricey off-the-peg henhouses here, but a children's playhouse, bought from eBay for £50 and painted by the kids. The 'nesting boxes' are simply an old bunk-bed ladder laid down flat, the gaps filled with wood shavings. Perches for the hens to roost on at night are pieces of wood screwed into the corner on a diagonal. The 5m x 3m run at the end of the garden is actually a fruit cage – the netting removed and replaced with weld wire that Olivia attached to the poles with cable ties and extended under the floor of the cage to deter digging from foxes.

Last summer they opened a hen hotel for all the local henkeepers to bring their hens to when they went on holiday. 'The kids made feeding menus and signs saying "shared accommodation" and "private rooms available". Hens are a commitment,' she says, 'but no more than having any pet. It's fun, like playing "farm".'

tip If you don't want to get up to let your hens out in the morning, it's worth investing in an automatic pop hole door opener when you buy your henhouse.

tip Do your neighbours a favour: don't get a cockerel. They aren't necessary for hens to lay eggs.

what other equipment do I need to keep hens?

Apart from the henhouse and run, you will need feeders and drinkers, bedding (horse bedding or straw – not hay, because it can make them ill), feed (layers pellets are easiest, mixed corn for an afternoon treat) and mixed grit to help your hens grind their food. A dustpan and brush, paint scraper, gloves and disinfectant are also essential to clean out the henhouse. A metal dustbin with a lid placed inside the run (if it's large enough) is useful as a secure place to keep the feed.

hens on the roof?

In a city environment where space is at a premium, rooftops are great spots for hens. But make sure you provide shade and shelter. Hens were originally jungle birds and roofs tend to be very exposed. Up high, they are safer from predators (though don't underestimate the fox's ability to climb).

what about my precious vegetable plants?

Yes, hens will eat your garden plants and vegetable crops if you don't protect them. But they will also eat your slugs and snails too, and they make lovely gardening companions. Protect individual new seedlings with cloches, cages or plastic fruit crates you can beg from the greengrocer. If you grow your vegetables in raised beds, it's easy to place a mesh cover over the top made of weld wire. With new trees or shrubs place stones around the base to stop the hens damaging the roots.

tip Hens prefer eating plants that are attached to the ground so why not give your hens a living salad by sowing fast-growing chard, lettuce, spinach or other leafy salads in plastic fruit crates? When the plants are about 20cm high put the crate in the run for the hens to graze on. Remove it before they can damage the roots and the plants should resprout a couple of weeks later.

how to MAKE A HEN-PROOF CLOCHE FOR FREE

you will need

A large plastic bottle such as a soft drink or mineral water bottle

Scissors or a craft knife

2 thin sticks from the garden, or chopsticks

10 minutes

when to do it

Any time of year

how to do it

Cut the bottom off the bottle. Remove the lid. Cut two slits in the bottle facing each other about 3cm up. Place your new cloche over a vulnerable plant and push the sticks through the slits and deep into the ground so the bottle can't be pushed over by your foraging fowl.

tip Don't throw away the bottom of the bottle you cut off. It's perfect for popping under pots to stop your windowsills getting soggy.

5

WEEDS HENS LIKE

Chickweed (see page 124)
Dandelions (see page 124)
Fat hen
Goosegrass (see page 124)
Nettles (see page 128)

KEEP... QUAIL

Members of the pheasant family, these placid little game birds lay an egg a day and don't need much space so make surprisingly good urban livestock. Don't let them out of their run, though, or you won't see them for dust. Unlike chickens, they are very strong flyers. Although they don't tend to exhibit the personality of hens or comic value of splashing ducks, quail are pretty, delicate-looking birds who can become quite tame once they get used to you. Their tiny speckled eggs – about a third the size of a hen's egg, and expensive to buy in the shops – are delicious eaten lightly boiled with asparagus, hard-boiled in salads, made into little Scotch eggs, pickled or used in baking. Give them away to friends and they will be mightily impressed. If you can bear to dispatch the little birds, their meat is also a delicacy. Expect your quail to live for between two and three years and lay eggs from six weeks old.

where can I buy quail?

Look for adverts in specialist poultry magazines or smallholding websites and fairs. Or try an online search. As with any livestock, check carefully before buying, preferably seeking local breeder recommendations on online forums.

what breed?

Most domesticated quail available to buy are Japanese quail, Chinese Painted, Italian quail or Cortunix quail.

what do they eat?

Quail will eat mashed up chicken layers pellets, corn and scraps from the kitchen. Preferred delicacies to be given in moderation include pasta, cake, rice, sweetcorn and lettuce. They will also eat some garden weeds such as chickweed and fat hen and particularly like eating blackfly so throw in your infested broad bean tops and they will be very happy.

where should I keep them?

Quail can't be free range like chickens since they will fly away. There are some specially made quail enclosures available to buy – the urban-styled company Omlet has a quail Eglu for six quail with a 2 x 1 metre run attached – but many people customise a rabbit hutch and combine it with a predator-proof run (a hen run for three to four chickens is ideal). If using a rabbit hutch, remove the wooden back panel and replace with weld wire since quail prefer a lighter environment than rabbits. Most rabbit hutches have a separate nesting area – again, this should be removed for quail since they won't need it. Use wood shavings on the floor and place a tray or ice cream tub of dry sand in the cage as a dust bowl – the quail love to bathe in it. Provide a rabbit drinker and a chicken feeder for water and food. Unlike chickens there is no need to lock your quail up in the house at night as long as they are safe from predators in their run.

One thing to remember with quail is that they fly directly upwards when alarmed. Every time you open the door, they can do this and if they gather speed when flying upwards they can hurt themselves on the roof of the run. For this reason, either keep them in a run less than 75cm high so they can't gain enough speed to hurt themselves or one that is at least 1.8m high so they don't hit their heads.

how many quail should I keep?

An average rabbit hutch (about 120cm x 60cm) would comfortably house six to eight quails. Most people include a couple of male birds in the mix because quail are social birds and like the dynamics of a family.

what other care do they need?

Clean them out once a week and move the quail house around the garden every couple of weeks to allow the grass to recover. Expect to spend about an hour and a half a week looking after your quail – an hour cleaning them out and a couple of minutes each day replacing their food and water and collecting the eggs. Their manure is dry and can be sprinkled on the garden as a fertiliser.

KEEP... DUCKS

The endearing, enduring image of Beatrix Potter's Jemima Puddleduck keeps these waterfowl high in people's affections, but ducks as city animals? Surely not?

In fact, a pair of ducks can be perfectly good livestock for a city garden. They are sociable, lay lots of rich eggs which are delicious in baking, will keep your garden slugs and snails to a minimum and are much less prone to diseases and mites than hens. Friendly and comical looking, they are trusting animals who will come running and eat out of your hand. They are also good guard ducks who will quack at intruders.

The smaller breeds don't even need a pond. As long as ducks have somewhere to bathe and wash, they are content. The bottom half of a plastic paddling pool, a wheelbarrow or a selection of plastic tub trugs filled with fresh water will have them splashing about happily.

how many ducks should I get?

Like chickens, ducks are sociable animals, so will get lonely on their own. Buy a minimum of two ducks. Most pure-breed ducks are sold as pairs – a drake (male) and a duck (female).

how much space do I need to keep ducks?

A pair of small ducks need approximately 7m x 8m of space. Two larger birds will need a minimum of 12m x 12m. They need access to water to splash in and ground to run around in. If your garden is big enough, fence them into an area so you can move them about every few weeks, allowing the grass to recover.

won't they turn my garden into a smelly mudbath?

Yes and no. Ducks like to dabble in the water, splashing about and making a mess of the ground around it. If you have a clay soil, it is likely to get very muddy, while sandy soils stay relatively pristine. In dry spells, your garden won't be too squelchy, but over winter when it's persistently wet, you can say goodbye to your lawn. Surrounding ponds/paddling pools with gravel will prevent it getting too muddy. Duck poo is messy but it will fertilise your soil.

I don't have a pond. How do I give my ducks access to water?

Plastic children's paddling pools make great splashing and bathing pools for urban ducks. Change the water every two weeks. The body part of a plastic wheelbarrow is also ideal. Prop objects around it so that the ducks can get in and out easily. Plastic tub trugs with handles, particularly the wide, shallow ones, can be spaced about the garden for plenty of splashing options. These are all light enough to move about the garden so you don't end up with just one muddy area.

are ducks noisy?

Female ducks quack. Male ducks squawk when handled. It's best to warn your neighbours before you commit to buying ducks. Campbell and Indian Runner ducks are the quietest breeds while Call ducks can, as their name suggests, make quite a racket.

are their eggs tasty?

Ducks are prodigious layers, with some breeds laying as many as 300 blue or white eggs per year though, like pure-breed hens, they tend to stop laying over winter. Duck eggs are richer than hens' eggs, ideal for baking or quiches.

best urban breed?

Pretty Call ducks, no bigger than a pigeon, are a good size for urban gardens, but their extremely loud quack might put you off. Also small, Miniature Appleyards, are quieter and lay between 100 and 180 eggs a year. Medium-sized Campbells (both Khaki and White) have an upright posture, lay about 200 eggs a year and are quiet and placid. They do not fly. Indian Runner ducks (of Jemima Puddleduck fame), with their tall upright bodies, make hilarious pets, running around looking like walking bottles – they lay around 150 eggs a year and come in different colours from chocolate to fawn and apricot.

what do ducks eat?

Ducks will eat all the slugs and snails in your garden, though unfortunately also the goldfish in your pond, if you have one. On the plus side they will eat the mosquito larvae in your pond too. They will also forage for worms. On a daily basis, they eat layers pellets, kitchen scraps, grass and garden weeds. Since they have a bill not a beak, they can't peck at food, so chop up scraps first.

won't they eat all my precious garden plants?

As long as they are well fed on household scraps and pellets, damage should be limited to the odd plant. You can always net individual plants to protect them.

are they vulnerable to predators?

Yes, very. Urban foxes will finish them off if they get half a chance so protect as you would for hens (see page 146). Some breeds may need their wings to be clipped to stop them flying away. Lock your ducks up at night in a duck house – plenty of options are available online – and let them out every morning. Many people let their ducks roam freely around the garden during the day, particularly if they can keep an eye on them. But if you are out, it's a good idea to fence off a secure area so they are safe from foxes.

KEEP... BEES

Unless you've had your head in a honey jar for the past 10 years, you'll know that the world's bee population is in a spot of trouble. You'll also know that, since bees pollinate about a third of our food, we could be in trouble too. Between 2006 and 2009, 35 per cent of US bees were wiped out. In 2008 alone, 35 per cent of Europe's 13.6 million honeybees died, and the UK honeybee population has halved in the past 25 years. Whether the blame can be laid at the door of agriculture – recent evidence linking insecticides to colony decline is startling (see page 98) – varroa mite, fungal disease or colony collapse disorder, one thing is certain: bees need help. And they're finding it in an unlikely place – the city.

From Brooklyn to Hong Kong, Paris, London, Amsterdam and Berlin, hives are turning up on rooftops and gardens. Membership of the British Beekeepers Association has doubled in the past three years. There are now about 12,000 hives in Greater London. Since New York City lifted the beekeeping ban in 2010, the number of beekeepers there has quadrupled with around 400 hives now located in the city. The Melbourne City Rooftop Honey project has put 40 hives on the Australian city's restaurants, hotels and cafés, and has plans for many more.

So firmly have bees now taken their place in the urban spotlight that designers at the Dutch electronics company Philips have come up with an indoor beehive so you can watch your bees at work from your own sitting room. The orange-tinted-glass Urban Beehive hangs inside the house with a hole in the outside wall for the bees to fly out. A pull cord activates smoke to calm the insects when you need to open the pod. It's still a prototype, but it makes you wonder if we might see these dotting the sides of our urban apartment buildings in years to come.

The new generation of urban beekeepers is not just in it for the honey. Beekeeping has suddenly gone from being the staid rural hobby of the 'beardos' (as one young beekeeper calls them) to a thriving environmental movement. Urban beekeepers see their hobby as part of a greater interest in sustainability; the honey is almost a bonus.

Honeybees like cities. Whichever metropolis you're in, the chances are that it has fewer insecticides than agricultural land and lots of rooftops safe from predators or vandals. While honeybees in the countryside might have to make do with acres of oilseed rape, city bees have a patchwork of gardens, windowboxes, street trees and parks at their disposal, filled with a variety of flowers. This makes for a richer-flavoured, more complex honey. Since cities are a few degrees warmer than rural areas, they get that nectar and pollen for longer in the year, too.

City bees must be happy because, according to some urban beekeepers, they tend to make more honey than their rural counterparts. The beehives on the roof of the Palais Garnier in Paris make 30kg of honey a year which, according to the proud beekeeper Nicolas Geant is twice what rural bees would make. In Berlin, beekeeper Erika Mayr boasts of gathering a staggering 40kg per colony – about 180 jars of honey per hive.

Of course, the more urban bees we introduce, the further the nectar they feed on has to go round, so it's more important than ever to plant lots of bee-friendly flowers in parks, rooftops, gardens and even windowboxes in the city. But it's hard to see this as an onerous task. Beekeeping demands some commitment and initial set-up costs, but you can expect sweet rewards and only the occasional sting for your trouble. As long as you get the right training, anyone with a small garden or rooftop can keep bees, and the contented low hum of a hive makes a great antidote to urban stress. Checking on a hive in a quiet secluded corner or high up above the traffic reminds you to be calm, to slow down. If you ever need reminding that there is more going on than your little troubles, try looking in a beehive. There's a whole world in there.

why keep bees in the city?

1 They're fascinating to watch.

2 They make delicious honey with a fuller, more complex flavour than rural honey.

3 You'll be protecting the global honeybee population.

4 Cities are good places for bees because they're full of diverse flowering plants for much of the year, low on insecticides and have lots of out-of-the-way rooftop spots perfect for siting hives.

5 It could help your hayfever. It is believed that eating a spoonful of local honey each day introduces local pollens to your body, making you less allergic to them.

so you want to keep bees...

what equipment do I need?

Apart from bees and a couple of hives (it is best to start with two so you can compare the way the colonies behave and have a back-up colony should things go awry), you'll need a smoker, a hive tool to extract the frames, protective clothing and gloves. You can buy the clothing (either a full suit or a hat and veil) secondhand and special gloves are not necessary – rubber washing-up gloves are fine.

can I just buy bees over the internet?

No. Before you buy anything, you must go on an introductory beekeeping course to get a feel for it. Look on the internet for your local city beekeeping group. Ideally, you should also be mentored for a year when you start beekeeping so try to find a local beekeeper you can shadow. Bees aren't for everyone – you will get stung at some point – and they behave differently throughout the year, so be sure this is the hobby for you before you commit. It's essential to join your local beekeeping association, which will be able to advise you of a good source for equipment and bees.

what will the neighbours say?

Wherever you keep your bees, talk to all your neighbours about it first to check that nobody has any serious allergies or objections. Once they know they won't be in the direct flight path, neighbours are usually more intrigued than alarmed. Offers of free honey always help.

Do I have time to keep bees?

During autumn and winter, expect to spend about an hour a week checking that the entrance is unblocked and that the bees have enough food. During the spring and summer, feeding the bees with sugar solution, checking the supers (the frames that hold the cones) and keeping varroa in check will take a couple of hours a week. Expect to harvest the honey once in July.

how much honey will I get?

A typical urban hive will produce about 30 x 450-g jars of honey a year.

how do I extract the honey?

You can rent extracting equipment from your local bee club or borrow from another member. Beginners will probably need help with the initial extraction and bottling and should ask a more experienced member.

won't I get stung?

All beekeepers get stung now and then, but honeybees aren't aggressive. As long as you don't tip over the hive or stand directly in front of the entrance, the bees will pretty much ignore you.

where should I put the hive?

Once you've placed your hive, you shouldn't move it again, so think carefully before deciding on a location. Bees need a secure spot where they won't be troubled by vandalism. Choose somewhere dry – bees hate the damp – and, if possible, position the hive so that the entrance faces south but doesn't point towards any houses.

the best spots for city hives

Your roof

The flat roof of your house or the gulleys between sloping roofs are ideal for hives since they are usually sheltered and out of the way of predators and other people. Flat garage or shed roofs are good too. On the downside, roof hives may not be easy to reach (particularly with heavy equipment) so check access is good first. Beehives should not be sited on a roof any higher than a large tree.

In your garden

Ideal if you can guarantee the security of the hive. Put a fence around the hive if you have children or dogs, and be careful not to put hives under trees in case the branches drop on them.

On your balcony

Balconies can be excellent locations for city beehives as long as you have enough space and your balcony is no higher than a large tree (any higher than this and the bees get too tired to forage successfully). You'll need a 60cm square for the footprint of the hive plus room to work around it as you unstack and restack it to check on the brood, the queen and the honey. Make sure the front of the hive faces away from your home and that there is at least 30cm between the entrance of the hive and any solid barrier so the bees can come in and out easily. Expect it to feel rather cosy, though, and visitors might be alarmed to see a buzzing box at the end of your balcony. Not one for the bee shy.

LEFT: During spring and summer, check the supers regularly.
BELOW: Rooftops are ideal spots for urban bees as long as they are no higher than a large tree.

what do I do if my bees swarm?

All bee colonies will swarm when the population reaches a certain size. The old queen flies off taking half the colony with her. It's a natural behaviour to increase the total bee population, but in cities, a cluster of bees hanging off a tree, roof or even motorbike engine tends to put people off their lattes. With experience you'll find that there are things you can do to deter swarming, such as clipping the queen's wings or dividing the colony when it looks like a swarm is imminent. Beginners faced with a swarm can call their local beekeeping group for help, but they should really know about swarm control and collection before taking on bees. A good beekeeping course should get you up to speed.

what about diseases?

The biggest challenge for beekeepers is keeping the varroa mite under control, as it is present in all colonies to some extent. Foul brood and colony collapse disorder are other concerns to contend with. Beekeepers need to be able to spot diseases, some of which are notifiable by law, and administer medication through the year. Local beekeeping groups can help with these problems.

can I sell my honey?

You don't generally need a licence to package and sell honey because it's a pure, natural food. If you are just selling 'from the door', to friends and local contacts, then you'll need to label the jar clearly, including your name and address, the net weight of the honey, best-before date (two years after bottling), country of origin and batch number. You must also keep a record of any medications you have administered to your bees. But each country has its own labelling requirements so be sure to check with your local beekeeping group. Then put up a sign by the front door. Don't forget to give your neighbours some free jars. As with any foodstuff that is sold, the area where it is prepared must be hygienic and the authorities will have the right to inspect your premises.

6 THINGS YOU MIGHT NOT KNOW ABOUT BEES

In its lifetime (which is about six weeks), an average worker bee will make a twelfth of a teaspoon of honey.

A typical hive contains 35,000–50,000 bees.

Despite the popular expression, bees don't have knees.

Bees can't see red.

Honeybees don't hibernate over winter: they huddle round the queen in a cluster the size of a football, dislocating their wings and flexing their muscles to keep warm.

A worker bee has to visit 1,500 flowers to make one drop of honey.

RURBANITE: Camilla Goddard, urban beekeeper, London

Camilla Goddard used to work at Sotheby's, the London auction house. These days, the former modern art consultant is putting on an installation of her own – in beekeeper garb and carrying a smoker – generally up on a roof. The bees in the 30 hives she looks after enjoy some of the most privileged locations and views in the capital, from the roofs of luxury hotels to the Soho flat of an award-winning film producer, a Covent Garden beauty store and the Garrick Club, where the hives are in club colours of salmon pink and cucumber green. After all, the author AA Milne was a former member, and what better use for the money he left the club than honey to delight Winnie the Pooh? Over in Greenwich, she has four hives in the fenced-off environs of Captain Hardy's tomb – of Admiral Nelson's 'Kiss me, Hardy' fame. You feel her beehives should all be wearing blue plaques.

So what's the appeal for her? 'You're totally connected to the seasons, and to your local environment,' says Camilla, who is studying to be a master beekeeper. Bees forage on whatever is around them. 'In spring you get light honey with an elderflower smell when you open the hives and I've had minty honey too. As the summer goes on, the honey gets darker. By looking at the colour of the pollen on the bees' legs, you can know what flower they've been foraging on.'

> 'Cities are good for bees because there are fewer insecticides.'

Why does she think more city people are keeping bees? 'It's very much part of the cycle of things if you're into growing your own,' she says. 'I think people do it for sustainability. Cities are good for bees because there are fewer insecticides. In London these days some people don't even harvest the honey at the end of the year, they just want to help the bees for environmental reasons.'

It's all worth it: even being called out at any time of day to rescue an errant swarm lodged 6m up a chimney! Camilla believes eating honey from her bees has cured her hayfever. In spring, she makes sure she holds back a few of the 60 jars she makes per hive to provide an important local service: 'I get all these hayfever sufferers sniffing down the phone so I keep some back for May.'

Camilla's tips for bee beginners

1 Start with a National hive (or Langstroth) and a small nucleus colony from a reputable source.

2 It takes some time for you and the bees to get to know each other so don't give up if you get stung at the beginning. You'll get patient and so will the bees.

3 Start with a new colony of bees at the beginning of the year. Beehives and bee-suits are expensive so put them on your Christmas list, and then you'll be ready to go early in the year.

4 Join a local club and internet forums.

5 It's okay to make mistakes.

buzzing on candy

In 2011 Brooklyn beekeepers noticed their bees were
returning with glowing red stomachs. Tests showed
that it was Red Dye no 40. It transpired that they were
foraging at the Dell Maraschino Cherries factory one
block away. They're not the only bees with a taste for
confectionery: a Long Island beekeeper who lived next
to a candy factory reported watching his bees create
a rainbow of high-fructose corn syrup – red, blue and
green – in their hive.

the flavour of the city

As the global urban beekeeping trend takes hold, city
hive enthusiasts are developing their own national
styles. Michael Leung became Hong Kong's first urban
beekeeper in 2010, with hives on towerblock roofs in
this built-up city. The Chinese approach to beekeeping
uses no protective clothing (no gloves and no head
nets) and no smoke. 'This gives us a closer connection
to the bees and disturbs them as little as possible,' he
says. 'When we work with them, we make sure it's a
sunny day and we move very slowly.'

In Brooklyn, a new generation of urban
homesteaders is finding something almost spiritual in
the slow buzz of beekeeping. 'Being a beekeeper has
given me a real sense of purpose. That's my religion, it's
what keeps me sane,' claims 30-something Megan Paska
who keeps several hives on rooftops in the city. Jars of
local honey are in hot demand at the farmers' markets.

Annette Muller, whose company Berliner Honig
sells honey from 500 beekeepers in Berlin, hopes that
her fellow citizens will start treating their city honey
as a gourmet foodstuff. Honey from each city will
have a unique flavour that's dependent on the city's
flora. 'It's going to become a product like wine or
cheese that people savour and discuss,' she says, 'where
people appreciate when, where, how and by whom it
was produced.'

FURTHER READING AND RESOURCES

BOOKS

Farm City: the Education of an Urban Farmer
by Novella Carpenter
(Penguin Press, 2009)

The Edible Balcony by Alex Mitchell
(Kyle Books, 2011)

The Edible Garden by Alys Fowler
(BBC Books, 2010)

Veg Street by Naomi Schillinger
(Short Books, 2013)

*The Living Garden – A Place that Works
with Nature* by Jane Powers
(Frances Lincoln, 2011)

The Wildlife Gardener by Kate Bradbury
(Kyle Books, 2013)

*Small Green Roofs – Low-Tech Options
for Greener Living* by Nigel Dunnett,
Dusty Gedge, John Little and
Edmund C Snodgrass

*Back Garden Seed Saving: Keeping Our
Vegetable Heritage Alive* by Sue Stickland
(Eco-Logic Books, 2001)

WEBSITES

rootsimple.com
Online presence for urban homesteaders
Kelly Coyne and Erik Knutzen. Plenty
of practical info here, from canning to
cropping

projectdirt.com
Vibrant hub for all things green and
urban, connecting like-minded souls and
informing them on all kinds of rurban
living, from green roof workshops to
community gardening and beekeeping

Landshare.net
Connects would-be food growers without
land with those who have land to share

farmlondon.weebly.com
'Eco-social design practice' bringing
farming to the city. Initiatives to inspire
rurbanites and events at the urban farming
hub farm:shop in Dalston, east London

theediblebusstop.org
Volunteer-based project turning neglected
areas along London's bus network into
productive community gardens

Prinzessinnengarten.net
The Berlin city farm in which everything
is grown in containers

What-if.info
Social regeneration project bringing food
gardens to neglected areas of the city

Brooklynhomesteader.com
Megan Paska's online treasure trove of
urban homesteading know-how

Verticalveg.org.uk
Useful site dedicated to growing
vegetables in tiny spaces

Bumblebeeconservation.org
The Bumblebee Trust website: great for
ID-ing different types of bumblebee in
your garden or out and about

Guerrillagardening.org
Richard Reynolds' web page uniting
guerrilla gardeners worldwide

Thepansyproject.com
Artist Paul Harfleet records his planting
of pansies at the site of homophobic
attacks in cities in The Pansy Project

Treesforcities.org
International charity Trees for Cities is
dedicated to planting trees in urban
areas

thepotholegardener.com
Browse miniature gardens made in city
potholes by photographer Steve Wheen

Thelondonorchardproject.org
Initiative that plants orchards in urban
areas and arranges urban fruit harvests

communitygarden.org.au
A network that connects community
gardens and gardeners around Australia

vegout.asn.au
An organic, chemical-free garden run
by volunteers in Melbourne

ecomatters.org.nz/community
Help and advice for starting a
community garden

garden.geek.nz
Emily Davidow's enthusiastic garden
experiments and explorations in
New Zealand

SUPPLIERS

sedumgreenroof.co.uk
Suppliers of small areas of sedum
blanket for DIY projects such as the
bird table roof

Wildflowers.co.uk
Online store for British Wildflower Plants,
ready-to-plant wild flower plugs that are
great for green roofs

Habitataid.co.uk
One-stop online shop for wildlife/
environmentally friendly plants and
equipment

realseeds.co.uk
Great source for heritage vegetable seed

Seedsofitaly.com
Online supplier of Franchi seeds –
generous packets of vegetable seeds
with an Italian flavour

Blackmoor.co.uk
Blackmoor Nurseries' online store – great
for fruit trees and edible hedging plants

Otterfarm.co.uk
Online supplier of edible plants and seeds
with an emphasis on the unusual

Reallywildflowers.co.uk
Suppliers of UK-provenance wild
flower seed

Pictorialmeadows.co.uk
Where to buy pictorial meadow seed

watersidenursery.co.uk
Good source for pond plants

Wigglywigglers.co.uk
Compost bins, wormeries and more

ecoseeds.co.nz
Offering a range of vegetable, herbs and
flower seeds for optimum organic growing

www.greenpatchseeds.com.au
Organic seed supplier

find

BOOKS

The Thrifty Forager by Alys Fowler
(Kyle Books, 2011)

River Cottage Handbook No 7: Hedgerow
by John Wright
(Bloomsbury, 2010)

The Forager Handbook by Miles Irving
(Ebury Press, 2009)

*The Wild Flower Key – How to Identify
Wild Flowers, Trees and Shrubs in Britain and
Ireland* by Francis Rose
(Warne, 1981)

Wild Flowers of Britain and Europe
by W Lippert, D Podlech
(Collins Nature Guides, 1994)

Wild Flowers by Sarah Raven
(Bloomsbury, 2011)

Wild Flowers of Britain by Roger Phillips
(Macmillan, 1977)

Weeds by Richard Mabey
(Profile Books, 2010)

Field Guide to Australian Flowers by Denise
Greig
(New Holland, 1999)

Wild Flowers of Australia and Oceania by
Michael Lavelle
(Southwater, 2008)

APPS

The Urban Birder City Guide: London

The Field Guide to British Birds

Wild Flowers by Pierre-Olivier Templier

WEBSITES

Plantlife.org.uk
UK wild plant charity

ispot.org.uk
A website aimed at helping anyone
identify anything in nature

projectnoah.org
Forums for uploading photos and sharing
identifications of plants and wildlife

Buglife.org.uk
Europe-wide organisation dedicated to
conserving inverterbrates

Theurbanbirder.com
Site of city birdwatching expert David
Lindo, dedicated to the observation and
study of birds in the world's cities

urbanbirder.com.au
birdwatching and nature sound recording
in Melbourne, Victoria and Australia

abundancenetwork.org.uk
The Abundance Network organises the
harvesting of unwanted public fruit in
cities across the UK. Find out if there's a
group near you and join in

www.fruitshare.net
Matches would-be harvesters with city
fruit that would otherwise go to waste

Fallenfruit.org
Los Angeles-based collective raising
awareness of the fruit that goes to waste
in the city

**nhm.ac.uk/nature-online/life/plants-
fungi/postcode-plants/**
Discover native wildflowers in your area

Eattheweeds.com
Fun website full of foraging recipes

livelocal.org.au
help with wild-food foraging

imagoforest.com.au/rs_ev.html
A community mapping project to share
the joys of scrumping by identifying street
fruit trees

milkwood.net
Cultivating clean food, future farmers, right livelihoods and sustainable skillsets for urban and rural abundance...

foragersyear.wordpress.com
A Sydney girl's adventures in foraging

BOOKS

Keeping a Few Hens in Your Garden
by Francine Raymond
(Kitchen Garden, 1998)

Keeping a Few Ducks in Your Garden
by Francine Raymond
(Kitchen Garden, 2002)

Chickens, the Essential Guide to Choosing and Keeping Happy, Healthy Hens
by Suzie Baldwin
(Kyle Books, 2012)

The Urban Beekeeper, a Year of Bees in the City by Steve Benbow
(Square Peg, 2012)

WEBSITES

Henkeepersassociation.co.uk
Membership site for the Henkeepers' Association, full of information and tips

Lbka.org.uk
The London Beekeepers' Association – first port of call for any Londoner who wants to get their hands on a beehive

Waterfowl.org.uk
Useful site for info on keeping ducks

Cortunixcorneruk. forumotion.com
Quail-keeping forum

urbanhomestead.org
A resource for transforming an ordinary city home into a productive city farm with the goal of reducing a family's environmental impact and returning to a self-sufficient way of life

livinggreener.gov.au
Advice for keeping backyard chickens

urbanchickens.org
Since 2007, Urban Chickens has been dedicated to the practice of backyard chicken keeping in urban and suburban environments

chickensathome.co.nz
Supplying coops, runs, feed, and chickens and offering courses that cover everything you need to know about keeping chickens

urbanbees.co.uk
Bringing bees to the city. Training and educating people to become responsible beekeepers in an urban environment

greenurbanliving.co.nz
Site of landscape architect Janet Luke, dedicated to sustainable design, edible landscaping and permaculture and living a sustainable lifestyle in an urban environment

SUPPLIERS

omlet.co.uk
Online treasure trove for the modern urban hen, home of the Eglu chicken coop and run

Flytesofancy.co.uk
Beautiful wooden hen houses and runs

www.backyardchickencoops. com.au
Supplying top-quality chicken coops suitable for the Australian climate at affordable prices

www.chooks.co.nz
Hen houses and poultry supplies

INDEX

ACKNOWLEDGEMENTS

Thanks so much to Heather and Elly who helped me get this idea off the ground, and to Judith and Kyle for turning it into a proper book with their customary skill and patience. Thanks, as ever to Sarah for her beautiful photos and calmness. On the home front, thanks to Mum, Helen and Amy for helping with the kids so I could write for five minutes without being yelled at by a small child and, as ever, to Donna for reminding me to keep it all in perspective.

Most of all, though, I want to thank all the rurbanites who have inspired me to write this book by sharing their tips, time and energy with me – the guerrilla gardeners, urban farmers, hen keepers, beekeepers, foragers, wildlife keenos and flower spotters who see beautiful wildness beyond the Tarmac.

So big thanks to wildlife queen Kate Bradbury, quail lover Simon Suter, Mr Green Roof Dusty Gedge, Kate Howell for allowing me to dig up her lawn and Sarah Hews for letting me loose on her garden shed with a saw. Thanks to hen keepers Olivia Knight and Vera Lily, Camilla Goddard at Capital Bee for her great beekeeping tips, to Paul Green of Avant Gardening for giving me the community gardening big picture, wildlife balcony gardener Keith Reynolds at valiantveggie.wordpress.com and Angela Woods at the London Bee Keeping Association for casting her eye over the bee chapter. Thanks to urban birder David Lindo for showing me a new side of Wormwood Scrubs and Peter Llewellyn of the Wildflower Society (thewildflowersociety.com) for answering my wildflower questions so patiently. I am especially grateful to Penelope Greenhough of Pickling Peckham for her tour of the city's secret foraging spots and her follow-up tips and recipes.

Countless community gardeners have inspired me, such as Naomi Schillinger (outofmyshed.co.uk), Will Sandy and Mak Gilchrist of the Edible Bus Stop, Nina Pope and Karen Guthrie at Abbey Gardens (abbeygardens.org), Marie Murray and Brian Cumming at Dalston Eastern Curve Garden in east London (dalstongarden.org) and the folk at Vacant Lot. Finally, thanks go to Francine Raymond and Jo Lewis for henkeeping advice and to Kate Lonergan of blackheathwindowbox.co.uk for her windowbox tips, veg grower Caro Shrives, fellow Deptford guerrilla Helen Russell and my Manhattan weed correspondent Steve Andrews.

PICTURE CREDITS

Published in Great Britain in 2013 by
Kyle Books
67–69 Whitfield Street
London
W1T 4HF
www.kylebooks.com

ISBN: 978-0-85783-072-2

10 9 8 7 6 5 4 3 2 1

Editor Judith Hannam
Assistant Editor Vicki Murrell
Designer Carl Hodson
Copy Editor Helen Griffin
Prop Stylist Ali Allen
Proofreader Anne Newman
Index Helen Iddles
Production Nic Jones, Gemma John and Lisa Pinnell

Text © 2013 Alex Mitchell
Design © 2013 Kyle Books
Photography © 2013 Sarah Cuttle
Except for: see picture credits on p. 175

Alex Mitchell is hereby identified as the author of this work in
accordance with section 77 of the Copyright, Designs and
Patents Act 1988.

A Cataloging in Publication record for this title is available at
the British Library.

Colour reproduction by Alta Image
Printed and bound in China by C & C Offset Printing Co. Ltd

Important note to readers
This book contains information on herbs and remedies that can be
used medicinally. It is not, however, intended as a medical reference
book. Before trying any remedies, herbal or otherwise, the reader is
recommended to sample a small quantity first to establish if there
is any adverse or allergic reaction. The reader is also advised not to
attempt self-treatment for serious or long-term problems without
consulting a qualified doctor. Neither the author or the publisher
can be held responsible for any adverse reactions to the recipes,
recommendations or instructions contained herein, and the use of
any remedy or herbal derivative is entirely at the reader's own risk.